AMEND A BROKEN MIND

A Memoir

William G. Richards

WILLIAM & JAMES PUBLISHING

Amend a Broken Mind
Published by William & James Publishing
581 Washington St, #3
South Easton, MA 02375

All right reserved. Except for brief excerpts for review purposes, no part of this book may be reproduced or used in any form without written permission from the publisher.

ISBN 978-1-940151-02-1

© 2020 William Richards
Editor: Aileen Richards

Printed in the United States of America
First Edition 2020

TABLE OF CONTENTS

Introduction 5
1 – Straight Line To Repentance 7
2 – Unexpected Change in Direction 40
3 – Into the Pit 54
4 – Revelation 74
5 – Sean's College Career 86
6 – Life with Sobriety 96
7 – Angels Everywhere 112
8 – Oxycontin 120
9 – I Want to Die 136
10 – Decision Time 152
11 – Meditation's the Answer 162
12 – Law School 174
13 – Homeless 198
Bibliography 220

INTRODUCTION

The story you are about to read is true. The names of people and of places have been changed to protect the privacy of everyone involved. Over the years I started and failed to chronicle these events too many times to remember. Each false start collapsed to the power of the emotions that inescapably flood in on me with each effort.

It is interesting to note, however, that I have shared the spoken form of this story or parts of it with my church youth group, one-on-one with people at NAMI meetings, state and county prisons, mental hospitals, and detoxification hospitals without many tears or any undue emotion. However, when I sat down to put it to paper, I would inevitably succumb to the emotions that were present during each event that is related.

The memories have receded somewhat with time. In a way, it is like the Doppler effect where the sound of a thing coming toward one has a higher pitch than the sound of the same thing going away. As the events related in this story happened their force on my life was considerable. However, as time passes the memory of the emotions associated with the event are moderated and less emotion is generated in the recollection

Notwithstanding, it is finally done, and I have benefitted greatly from the telling. I pray that it shows in the text. I pray that someone besides myself reads it.

AMEND A BROKEN MIND

This first edition has been edited by me dozens of times. My hope is that the language and form are enough to convey the lessons that I have learned, the growth that I have experienced, and the wonderful comfort that faith in a living God brings. One huge struggle that I had was keeping the order of events chronologically accurate. I think it is straightened out now. However, I apologize for any confusion that the reader may experience.

1 – STRAIGHT LINE TO REPENTANCE

It is December 2019 on Massachusetts' North Shore and the wind is cold and wet with sleet. I am walking on the beach at Plumb Island loving the feeling of the cold wind on my cheeks, the sound of the waves crashing on the shore, the sound of herring gull overhead and the smell of the sea. I come here when I need to work things out in my mind. I'm an old man now. I have lived the story you are about to read. In some ways, I am still living it. Age has given me the gift of perspective and patience. However, I am still looking for understanding. Patience and perspective are indeed gifts, but time is running out for understanding.

My name is Chad D'Amour. I was born in Massachusetts January 28, 1952 and have lived here all my life. 1952: the year of the first hydrogen bomb test on a hapless atoll in the Pacific; the year Polio was still rampant in the U.S. killing 3,300 people and crippling ten thousand others; and the year American boys were still dying in Korea in the fight against Communism.

My Mom and Dad were just regular folks, and both have passed away as of this writing. My Dad died first – after 60 years with my Mother. Mom grew up on a chicken farm in Bow, New Hampshire. Her mother and father came from Sweden. She went to local schools and graduated from nursing school in Concord, New Hampshire. My mother and her sister had a local radio show Sunday afternoon where they sang duets

AMEND A BROKEN MIND

and told jokes. After graduation and licensing as a nurse, she moved to Boston to work at Mass General Hospital.

My Dad's mother was French Canadian. His father was a U.S. Marine who went to college on the G.I. bill and became an economics professor at one of the many colleges in Boston. My Dad's mother died when he was young, and he spent a few years in a Catholic boy's school until his father got married again. While at the boy's school my Dad contracted polio. When he recovered sufficiently from the polio he moved in with his grandparents in Beverly, MA. He lived with Mamier and Papier who worked in the mills but spoke little English.

In a way, he was fortunate compared to other polio sufferers in his pre-vaccine generation. The only physical damage he suffered from the polio was in his left leg. It was slightly shorter than the other leg and much weaker so that he walked with a slight limp. It kept him out of Korea. However, the psychological scars were deep. Throughout his life he could not shake a feeling of loss and abandonment because of the early death of his mother and his father's decision to send him away to the boy's school.

My Dad had artistic abilities and eventually went to the Museum School of Art in Boston. He met my mother at a club in Boston and they got married. I was the first born of five children – three girls and two boys.

As our family grew, my parents could not support the family with Dad's art and Mom's part time nursing, so he got a job in

1 – STRAIGHT LINE TO REPENTANCE

Danvers, Massachusetts at a company that made light bulbs. He started out as a janitor. We lived across the street on the first floor of one of three white, three-story tenement buildings. The type you see all over Boston's north shore with porches on the back at each level and a stairway connecting each porch from bottom to top. The company maintained a glass dump across the street from the tenement buildings. My oldest sister and I lived surrounded by lots of other children whose parents worked at the same company.

The company encouraged their employees to improve their education and Dad took advantage of that program by attending Northeastern University evenings on the company's dime. He graduated with an engineering degree and he passed the test that gave him the PE moniker (Professional Engineer). The company promoted him to quality assurance manager and my parents were able to buy a new home in the next town over. This going to school nights and working days to get the company to pay for the education must have rubbed off on me because that is what I did when the time came.

My mother gave me the habit of thrift and honesty regarding money. She collected Green Stamps. I would go shopping with her during the summer because my sisters were at YMCA programs and I was at home alone with my mother. Before we went into the store, we would sit in the car in the parking lot and count the stamps she had collected. She had a dream to redeem those stamps for a new Singer sewing machine. It was redeemable with I don't know how many thousands of Green

Amend a Broken Mind

Stamps. After shopping and once the groceries were in the car, we would sit in the parking lot to make sure she got the stamps that she was entitled to relative to the money she spent on groceries. One day after we shopped, she noticed that the cashier had given her too much change. She looked over at me, saw me counting in her hand and it was obvious that I knew she had been given more cash than she should have been given. I could see her hesitate in her mind. We were quite poor having five children and only one income. She carefully counted every penny my father brought in. Looking at the coins in her hand with the pile of Green Stamps littering the seat between us she sighed and said, "I'll be right back."

I watched her walk into the store, saw her talking to the cashier, and further saw her hand back to the lady the incorrect portion of change.

I started first grade in the Beverly Public Schools. The only thing I remember on that first day of school was that I cried when my mother dropped me off. However, I eventually adjusted, and later that year my parents were convinced by the school that I should skip second grade.

Our new home was in a *cul d'sac* development of small cape-cod design houses. The neighborhood was full of children around my age and most of the boys were of Italian descent. We were the only French family in the neighborhood, but we were all being raised in the Catholic faith. In our free time, all the boys would get together to play baseball in the field down the

1 – STRAIGHT LINE TO REPENTANCE

street during the summer, football in the fall, hockey when the pond in the woods froze and basketball with a hoop on a telephone pole in between. We fought, played and grew up together. As you might expect, a lot of silly, dangerous and unkind things happened.

The development (a smaller version of the famous Levittown developments) was next to a stream and a swamp so, in the spring the rain usually flooded everything -- including the cellar of our home. My sister and I distracted ourselves by riding around the cellar on our bikes in the four inches of water from the rising water table. I bought my bike for 25 dollars earned shoveling driveways during the winter. The bike was a Schwinn cruiser to which I added a banana seat and high-rise handlebars. My sisters and I rode round and round the cellar laughing and screaming.

When the Fourth of July came around, one of the fathers in the neighborhood would drive to New Hampshire and buy fireworks for the kids in the neighborhood. With these explosives we dared each other to hold them in our hands while they exploded, dropped them lit into the mail boxes of neighbors, and ran laughing and howling into the night listening for the boom that would tell all the neighborhood that we were on the prowl.

We also exhibited our skill with knives by playing a game that required us to stand facing each other, feet about a foot and a half apart. We would then take turns throwing our knives

Amend a Broken Mind

between each other's legs. If no one got stabbed, we would bring our feet a little closer together and throw again. The game ended when one opponent chickened out first, the knife tip did not stick into the ground, or one of us got a knife stuck into our foot or ankle.

One afternoon we were playing this knife game when Stevie Vaspioni's father came out of his house very excited and said, "I used to play that game when I was a kid!"

He then took my knife and told his son Stevie to stand facing him. Stevie did what he was told and stood with his legs far apart. There were eight or ten of us boys there and we surrounded Stevie and his father. We watched enthralled as Stevie's dad commanded," Put your feet closer together! No, closer!"

Stevie, looking understandably dubious, was standing there with his feet about six inches apart when his father threw my knife at the space between his son's feet.

Now, my knife was a good throwing knife. It still is. I could throw it at a tree 10 feet away and it would stick in point first every time. However, when Stevie's dad threw the knife, he threw it inaccurately and too hard. It missed the space between Stevie's feet and stuck firmly into his instep.

Stevie was known among us kids as a fast-talking, storytelling, Italian boy who, when we laughed with incredulity

1 – STRAIGHT LINE TO REPENTANCE

at his wild stories, would spit on the ground and say," Bet you a dime," (spit), "bet you a dime" (spit), "bet you a dime!"

However, when my knife stuck into his instep, he let out a howl and hopped around on one foot in a spirited way with his father chasing him around yelling, "Stand still so I can pull it out!"

We watched with utter amazement and relived the moment with laughter and awe for months afterword. Stevie was so embarrassed he stopped hanging around with us and I didn't see him again until 25 years later when he was sitting on the bench as a district court judge hearing a motion that I argued before the court.

Another boy in the neighborhood had the last name of Rungus. When he came to the field to join in our games we would sing in chorus," Syringus, syrungus there must be a fungus among us – Rungus!"

He would throw a couple stones at us, swear at us for a while, and then join in on one of the teams. It never occurred to us that our mocking chorus might hurt him.

In the winter we would go sledding on the hills in the woods nearby, play basketball on the courts down the street (after we shoveled off the snow at the outdoor courts). In the summer we would play sandlot baseball morning, noon and night. Sometimes we would break into teams and go into the woods and play Swamp Fox, tag, hide and seek, or kick the can.

Amend a Broken Mind

Midsummer we would go to the blueberry fields and lay on our backs talking and eating blueberries.

My parents also had access to a cottage on Plumb Island's South end known as Sandy Point. We usually spent the month of August there. The cottage was located, along with five other cottages, on the Plumb Island Sound side of the island on a beach between 50-foot-high Bar Head and a peninsula a quarter of a mile north called Ipswich Bluff. The cottage had no running water. A squeaky hand pump in the kitchen supplied the potable water we needed. A hole in the sand out behind the cottage with a five-by-five-foot shack over it served as the toilet. An old potbellied, wood burning stove took the nip from the occasional chilly evening and served as the cooking stove. The cottage was balanced a few feet above the dunes on weathered posts gathered from the beach years before. At flood tide the sea came almost to the front steps. During a storm, the cottage was surrounded by the sea.

Except for shelves between the wall studs, the inside of the cottage was unfinished. The shelves were packed with thousands of paperback books and canned foods. However, there was little time for reading because the days were filled with fishing, swimming, boogie board surfing, snorkeling and roaming the dunes.

Outside the cottage was covered with weathered shingles. The whole place measured no more than 21 feet on each side. Infront, facing West across the sound toward Little Neck,

1 – Straight Line To Repentance

Ipswich was one huge, picture window. My parents slept on a convertible couch placed facing the picture window. My sisters and I took the partitioned areas in the back of the large, single room. Each of us had a bed that, no matter how hard we tried to prevent it, filled up with sand from the beach each night.

I had a seven-foot sailing dingy in which I spent a lot of my time sailing and fishing. One day I caught a striped bass almost as-long-as I was tall. On other days I would run into a school of mackerel or fill the boat up with flounder. Occasionally I would tie the painter from the dingy around my waist, put on a mask, snorkel and flippers and drift with the tide while holding a handmade spear in one hand. I was looking specifically for sharks. I never managed to catch one, but I did strike now and then with my lance. The lance just bounced off their tough hide and they would scoot away.

One day the wind was blowing briskly, and I was sailing up and down the sound. After a while I was getting bored, so I pulled the sail in tight, headed on a close reach and the boat capsized. I laughed as the boat went over. After righting the boat and getting the water out I sailed on until I got some good headway. Then I purposely capsized again. I repeated the sequence a couple more times when I looked up and saw my father approaching in our Boston Whaler. He yelled over the wind as he came alongside, "What are you doing? Are you in trouble?"

I smiled and yelled back, "No."

Amend a Broken Mind

He said, "Why are you capsizing?"

I smiled again and said, "It's fun."

He rolled his eyes and left me to my game.

After a while I got tired and hungry and pointed the bow to shore where I noticed an official state vehicle parked in front of the hermit's house down toward the point. Curious, I headed that way and ran my boat up on the beach.

The point was formed by sand accumulating around the base of a gravely hill that was left behind by the glaciers when they retreated 10,000 years-or-so ago. Each year the point would look different in the spring after winter storms sculpted the sand around the base of Bar Head. The hermit lived in a hollowed-out sand dune high above the flood tide mark that was supported inside by driftwood and outside by more driftwood tied together with leather strips. There was a door with leather hinges and two tusks standing upright on either side of the door. The tusks gave the place a spooky quality that attracted me and sparked my imagination. However, the reality was that the hermit was just a veteran who arrived after the Second World War and lived on his pension.

As I approached the hermit's hovel, I heard a very loud discussion between the State Representatives who were trying to issue the Hermit an eviction notice and the Hermit himself telling them to get off his property. I stood at a respectful distance and watched the Hermit gesticulate wildly as he yelled

1 – Straight Line To Repentance

at the State Representatives. He was dressed only in ragged, stained khakis. His hair was wild, mostly black but streaked with white. His skin was leathery and dark from years exposure to the sun.

The government people eventually left and, except for the wind and the lapping of waves on the beach, all was quiet once again. Our dinner of fresh, steamed, soft-shelled clams dug from the mud flats in front of the cottage and flounder that I caught that morning, along with a loaf of fresh bread that my mother magically produced in the wood stove was standard island fair.

The conversation at our table was not standard fare though. We talked about the Hermit and what his eviction meant to our future on the island. Our cottage had been on state land for many years – as-long-as the Hermit's hovel was anyway. It was always in the back of our minds that the State would one day evict us.

I, however, forgot about the hermit when, the next morning, I looked outside and a vehicle resembling a bread truck came chugging down the beach. The driver passed our cottage with the engine revving and the tires spinning in the sand. The van finally settled, unable to go any further, in the loose sand about fifty feet South of our cottage. The door to the back of the van opened and out hopped a cute young girl about my age.

Her family stayed on the island for the last two weeks in August and I got to know the young girl well enough to get my

Amend a Broken Mind

first kiss. At the end of their stay I worked hard to help them get their van out of the loose sand onto the firmer surface closer to the water. I was curiously saddened by their departure and the next morning at sun rise I saw the silhouette of a hunter with shotgun in hand standing on the top of a dune and knew that it was time for us to leave too. I had a premonition that something important was coming to an end. Just like for Adam in "Good Omens". The summer had ended, there would be other summers, but never one like this ever again.

You see, before we left the island for the summer, a group of uniformed men came to take the hermit away. After we returned home, we learned that he was emotionally disturbed and was taken to a veteran's home. Not long after, a letter came to us from the state explaining that we were to be evicted from our cottage just as the Hermit had been evicted from his. The State wanted to provide a haven for the endangered Plover shorebird, and we were in the way.

Returning home meant school was to start again and that fall, when I was not out playing in the woods and around the neighborhood, I spent hours in my room assembling balsa wood airplane and plastic car models. The air would get dense with toluene and acetone from the glue and cleaner that was used at the time. Then, as I got a little older, I started collecting elements like lead, mercury, tin, iron, calcium, carbon, boron, silicon, copper, potassium, magnesium, etc. My goal was to collect all the elements on the periodic table. Most were harmless. Some, like lead and mercury, were very dangerous for

1 – STRAIGHT LINE TO REPENTANCE

a child to handle. I liked to handle the mercury in my hands watching the dull grey, liquid metal pour from one hand to the other. The lead had a sweet taste, and, in my ignorance, I enjoyed sucking on it.

When I entered the sixth grade, I started experiencing feelings of anxiety and nervousness. I became irritable and would feel numb and weak at times. No one realized it but these were symptoms of mercury poisoning. I was also physically smaller than my classmates. My parents thought my small size was due to being moved ahead one year in the second grade. My inability to keep up with the schoolwork created a lot of tension at home and in school. My sixth-grade teacher frequently voiced disapproval of me out loud to the class. She accounted my poor academics and behavior problems to a bad attitude and laziness. I retreated inward and began a habit of avoidance – avoidance of adults, difficulties, and challenges.

Notwithstanding these things, I continued to be moved forward in the public-school system. The occasional teacher would spend extra time with me, and I would pass the necessary courses. One teacher in the 7th grade realized that I could not read and arranged to have me sent to a special class for non-readers.

These issues did not seem to interfere with my abilities to build my models and collect earth elements. As my element collection grew, I began to experiment. I taught myself about

Amend a Broken Mind

the periodic table, chemical bonding, chemical reactions, and radioactive elements. I met a kindred spirit in the eighth grade.

His name was Billy Pike. His parents adopted him when he was an infant. He was a little older than me and quite odd, but he was fascinated with my element collection and he liked to build models too. When I showed him how to make black powder, he was very excited. I never did anything with the powder other than set a match to a small pile of it and watched it flare up on a rock in the back yard. Billy, though, brought some of it home with him and packed it into a pipe, sealed the ends, and attached a fuse from a M80 firecracker. He demonstrated his creation one Sunday morning after church by burying it in a field and setting light to the fuse. The explosion created a 4-foot wide hole in the ground and stunned me. Someone called the police. However, we were gone before they arrived. I had no idea the black powder that I gave him was capable of such a blast.

Two weeks later he failed to show up at school. I didn't think much about it at the time. However, later that week my mother sat me down and asked questions about Billy and me. She was curious about what we did when we hung out together. She finally told me he had been arrested the previous weekend. He had blown a hole in the wall of the local Zayres department store with some of the black powder that I gave him and stole a television. For some reason that I will never know, he took the TV and hid in a camouflaged hole he had dug in the ground behind the store. That is where the police found him. Billy was

1 – STRAIGHT LINE TO REPENTANCE

arrested and I never saw him again. Years later my mother told me that he was sent to jail and a few years after that I heard that he was killed by another inmate.

I made another friend after Billy went away. His name was Cheever Blondski. He was three years older than me, a foot taller than me, lanky, and had slightly clubbed feet. He liked to wrestle with me and his nickname for me was "Stupid". "You are a lousy wrestler, Stupid." He would taunt.

"Hey, Stupid. I'll race you around the block," he would yell when he saw me coming.

We built a tree hut in the woods behind his house and once it was finished, we spent the night in it. The second night we slept in the tree hut I woke up with my pants down around my ankles and him on top of me poking his thing at my butt. I don't remember feeling anything – just him poking away while I laid there playing at sleeping. Eventually, he stopped, wiped my butt and pulled my pants up. The next day neither of us said anything but I felt odd. The thing was, I was lonely, and Cheever was the only friend I had. What I mean to say is that I spent a lot of time with Cheever as my only company. He would bring me into his room, get me naked and rub himself on me. Then, when his sister came home, he would go behind the wall to peak at her while she undressed. When he came back to his room, he would be acting weird, calling me names while he groped me and rubbed against me again. It was confusing.

Amend a Broken Mind

This activity repeated itself throughout the summer until school started. Cheever began to avoid me by leaving early to school and being unavailable after school. It was during this time that I began to sense that there was something wrong in my mind. I began to feel like there were two of me – a second distinct personality. I would sit alone in my room and try to do my homework. I liked the idea of doing well in school and working towards a goal. But this other personality interrupted my plans. He would fight me. Telling me I was a looser and the work was a waste of time.

As time went on my two personalities became more distinct. I wanted to be a good person, learn about new things, and make my parents proud. However, the second personality was a strong and provocative debater. He would often prevail, arguing that I was a looser, that I was stupid, that no matter what I did I would be misunderstood and in the wrong. He was also able to bring me outside of myself as if I was an observer looking down from above. I called him *le connard (asshole)*.

The first time I had an out-of-body experience outside of my room was when I was in ninth grade. I had a crush on a girl with whom I was afraid to approach. I thought I would break the ice by giving her a gift on her upcoming birthday. I went to Zayre's (the same one Billy blew up) and was looking around for something appropriate. I started to feel anxious and self-conscious when, suddenly, I realized that I was looking down upon myself from the store ceiling. It frightened me at first. But I watched as a saleswoman approached me to ask if I needed

1 – STRAIGHT LINE TO REPENTANCE

help. I could hear my soft voice tell her that I was looking for a gift for a girl my age. She pointed out a few things and I started to get very nervous and wanted to get out of there. So, I bought a pen stand with a bronzed bowler on it and left.

I never gave the girl the birthday present I bought that day. *Le connard* convinced me that it would be a stupid move, and she would reject me for being a weird-o. I mean, what did a bowling figure on a pen stand have to say about the feelings that I had for this girl? "Nothing", *le connard* argued.

Things happened outside my mind that supported the disparaging words of my second personality. For instance, in the 10th grade, I decided that I wanted to get a school jacket for sports achievement. There was a program where runners could post the distances they ran on a board and would work to run 100 miles in a year. I began to run on the indoor track at school as well as on the outside adding the distances to the board. A few weeks after I started running, I was confronted by the track coach. "D'amore," he said, "You have not run those distances that you posted."

I was taken aback with the accusation by an adult who had never spoken to me before. "Yes, I have." I replied defensively while studying my shoes.

Without another word, he turned and left me standing there. The next day I went to post my miles and my name had been removed from the board. That evening, in the quiet of my room, *le connard* reminded me that I was wasting my time

AMEND A BROKEN MIND

trying to accomplish anything. And I saw myself from above, sitting on my bed, tiny, helpless and alone.

A week later the school gym class consisted of a coed volleyball game. I was surprised because the gym classes always separated the girls and boys. The ball was put into play by the girls on the other side of the net and I positioned myself to return it. When I jumped up to hit the ball another boy on my team grabbed my shorts and pulled them down. I quickly pulled them up and chased him until I caught him and began beating the devil out of him. I just snapped. I straddled him, grabbed his head and banged it repeatedly on the cement. *Le connard* was in charge at that point. It was the first time in my life that I can recall feeling total, uncontrolled anger. I felt like I wanted to tear that boy apart limb by limb. It was like my anger was a raging fire that would not go out. I was able to bloody the boy before I was pulled from him. The result, I was suspended from school for a week.

Of course, my parents wanted to know what happened, so I told them about being de-panted during the coed volleyball game. I did not connect the volleyball game to the accusation of the gym teacher at that time nor did I connect the anger to the sexual abuse I experience. However, when my parents went to talk to the school officials, they were told that I had falsified the track records. Even though I insisted to my parents that I did run the miles -- they believed the school. *Le connard* laughed and his voice became louder – his personality more influential.

1 – Straight Line To Repentance

I tried to play baseball after this but was not allowed to take part in the practices and spent hours sitting on the bench. The coach had me sit or stand on the side lines until I gave up and stopped showing up. As I tried to find my place at the school, I also tried to ignore *le connard* whose voice kept getting louder telling me why bother. Finally, I joined the marching band, jazz band, and pep band where I played trumpet, French horn and E flat alto all of which I picked up quickly.

Activity in the band helped my attitude and quieted the voice some. I did find academic success in algebra and chemistry but graduated well down in the class overall. This was okay with me. I never thought that I would go on to further my education after high school. I was fed up with school and learned to distrust authority and just about everyone else too.

While learning to play an instrument and taking part in the various bands I started dating the girls in the marching band. After working my way through the list of available young women one at a time, I met a dark-haired flute player named Laurie. She was smaller than me and physically very nicely built. During that time the girls wore mostly short-short skirts and tight jerseys. Laurie had smooth legs, slim hips and largish breasts. I still remember the first time we went to the beach and she removed her jeans and blouse to reveal a two-piece bathing suit. Compared to today's standards it was modest, but she got my teenaged heart pumping that's for sure!

Amend a Broken Mind

I enjoyed spending time with her, and I thought we had something going. When we kissed, we would profess our love for each other. I tried very hard to be a gentleman as we called it back then. I never told her about *le connard*. He was telling me to get more aggressive sexually with her and made my life miserable when I was alone in my room thinking about her. Laurie and I even talked about getting married after high school.

One very rainy night I picked her up at her parent's house to go to a party. The guy hosting the party made sure his parents were gone and he provided plenty of booze. Laurie drank too much wine and got fall-down drunk. I did not drink at all that night and was vaguely disappointed in her, but I carried her to the car and buckled her into the front seat. On the way home she demanded I pull over so she could pee. I pulled over and she dropped her pants right next to the car and peed. Then she plopped back into the car seat with her pants around her knees. I said firmly as I stared out the front window in an effort not to ogle her nakedness," Laurie, pull your pants up."

She unbuckled her seatbelt and partially covered herself but when I told her to buckle her seat belt again, she stubbornly refused and yelled at me saying, "Stop bossing me around."

I realized I needed to get her home, but *le connard* said I should take advantage of the situation and take her parking some place. The debate began in my mind with me heading towards Laurie's home. However, before we reached her house and the argument in my mind reached a conclusion, a car

1 – STRAIGHT LINE TO REPENTANCE

crossed the center line in the road and hit us head on. Laurie, with no seat belt, lurched forward hitting the rear-view mirror, the front window and the passenger's side window before ending up an unconscious bloody mess on the car floor. I was uninjured because I was wearing a seat belt. In the eerie, post-accident quiet I called out, "Laurie, Laurie are you okay?"

She did not answer. I unbuckled my seat belt and ran to a house nearby. The occupant called for help. I went back to the car and tried to administer what first-aid I could. I used my t-shirt to stop the blood that was coming from cuts on her face. She was taken away in an ambulance, her pants still undone and not fully up, and my totaled car was towed from the scene.

I spent most of the night at the hospital feeling responsible. *Le connard* argued that if I had taken her parking like he wanted I would not have been in the wrong place at the wrong time. I had to admit he was right there. The harder I tried to do what was right the worse things seemed to get. To add insult to injury when I went to visit her the day after the accident the first words she said were, "You didn't do anything to me while I was drunk did you?"

Confused I asked, "What do you mean?"

She said, "You know." And pointed between her legs. "The nurse told me that my pants were undone and not all the way up when I arrived at the hospital."

Amend a Broken Mind

I said angrily, "No, I did nothing to you, but I did tell you to pull up your pants and buckle your seat belt after you took a piss."

Le connard laughed at me.

Laurie had to undergo plastic surgery on her face and, when her parents came to me to assure me that they knew the accident was not my fault and that they held no bad feelings toward me, *le connard* was pushing me to tell them, "If she had put her seat belt on like I told her she would not have been hurt."

However, I said nothing and when she got out of the hospital, Laurie and I went on a date in my new car. The first thing she did when she got in the passenger's seat was fasten her seat belt.

Our relationship started to go downhill from there. My best friend at that time was a guy named Charlie Hoite. We often went skiing together and it was with him that I skied Mount Washington from summit to base one spring after climbing from the AMC lodge at Pinkham Notch, up the trail to the headwall, up the side of the headwall across the snow fields to the summit.

As we were skiing across the snow fields coming down from the summit a dense fog bank rolled in. We could not see five feet in front of ourselves. Charlie and I began yodeling loudly back and forth to keep in touch with each other as we continued skiing in the dense fog. It was so exciting and totally awesome.

1 – STRAIGHT LINE TO REPENTANCE

The terrain was smooth snow fields with a few inches of recently fallen powder on top. All I heard was the sounds of the skis swishing through the snow with each turn and Charlie yodeling up ahead: No competing personality; no school administrators; no bullies.

Suddenly, Charlie yelled, "STOP!"

I stopped immediately kicking up a flying blanket of snow and laughing heartily. Slowly I shuffled on my skis toward Charlie's voice. As I did, I could hear other voices laughing and talking as clear as day. It was confusing, "Where the heck are we?" I yelled to Charlie.

When I came up to him I stepped out of the fog like walking through a door and I could see that we were at the top of the 800-foot vertical drop that is the Mount Washington Headwall – a large bowl like chunk carved out of the side of the mountain thousands of years ago by a glacier. The voices were from other skiers 800 feet below who were climbing the Headwall and Hillman's Highway just as we had earlier. We looked at each other and laughed.

Charlie said, "Can you imagine what it would have been like to go flying over this Headwall if we hadn't stopped in time?"

I laughed and shivered at the thought. We headed to the side of the Head Wall towards Hillman's Highway where an avalanche had provided a tolerably smooth slope. Charlie and I skied down the Hillman's Highway hooting and laughing all the

Amend a Broken Mind

way to the base camp a few miles away along the Sherborn Trail.

Skiing Mount Washington was in the spring of 1970, the year after my high school graduation. Later that summer, Charlie was riding his motorcycle on the main street in town when a car pulled out from a side street and hit him broadside. He only wore a helmet because it was the law and he never secured the buckle around his neck. The result was that when he got hit his helmet flew off and he hit his head on the street. I found out about his accident a week later from an acquaintance. The day I found out I went to visit him at the hospital. I had a skiing magazine that I bought for him with a cool article on skiing Mount Washington.

I was flummoxed by what I saw when I walked into his room. There was Laurie, my Laurie, laying on the bed with her arm and leg across Charlie's body. Snuggling up with him like she belonged there. I did not even know that they knew each other. However, as soon as Laurie saw me, she quickly moved away from Charlie. I looked from Laurie to Charlie and he just smirked at me. I tossed the magazine to him and left the room. I stopped seeing Laurie after that and when, a month later, I saw Charlie he laughed and said to me, "Hey, Chad. Guess what? I fucked Laurie."

I graduated high school when I was 17 and one week after graduation, but before Charlie's accident, my parents, who had been fighting a lot recently, split up. When my father stormed

1 – STRAIGHT LINE TO REPENTANCE

out of the house my mother called me downstairs and made me stand in the middle of the kitchen. She began beating me with a stick that she used to discipline us kids. When the stick broke against my hip, she took out a belt with a metal buckle. I guessed that she was angry because my father left. She was really getting into it with the belt, but I just stood there and took it not crying out like I had at this kind of treatment in the past. *Le connard* showed me the scene from above and I felt strangely peaceful as I took the beating and looked down on the spectacle. At one point, my eyes met my mother's eyes. She suddenly realized what she was doing, dropped the belt and said, "Go to your room Chad."

A week later I was upstairs in my room and my mother burst in holding my cousin Joey in her arms. He was blue in the face and not breathing. I took him from my mother and laid him on my bed. After clearing his passageways, I proceeded to apply mouth to mouth respiration (CPR was not available at the time). Joey quickly responded to my efforts. By the time the ambulance arrived he was his normal color and was breathing freely. Unfortunately, he stopped breathing again on the way to the hospital. He had a bad case of pneumonia and no one knew it.

That beating was not the first that I took for my father. And it wasn't the first time my mother called for my help to rescue a situation. The level of violence, yelling and arguing at home seemed to grow as we got older and my father's drinking got worse. One evening, I was in my bedroom praying fervently to

Amend a Broken Mind

God for help with waves of depression, loneliness, and the growing aggressiveness of the voice in my mind when suddenly I paused and looked up. Silence surrounded me. There was no response to my prayer. Out of the quiet, *Le connard* laughed, and I said out loud, "What am I doing? There is no God."

To add insult to injury, *le connard* stepped outside my body and showed me how pathetic I looked there on my knees, next my bed, with tears staining my face. With that, *Le connard* convinced me that I had only myself to rely on.

I was also convinced college would be more of the same crap I experienced in high school and I was not interested. After the beating in the kitchen and saving Joey's life, I went out and got a job at a computer company as a computer operator running payroll and printing checks for local companies. This was before the day of the personal computer and I was making enough money to afford a car and an apartment. What did I need college for?

The job made it possible for me to move out of my parent's house to an apartment first in West Gloucester and then down the street from my job near Derby Wharf in Salem, Massachusetts. The Salem apartment had two bedrooms on the top floor of a triple decker; like the one I lived in with my parents when I was an infant. The cool thing about the apartment was that the first floor held a Polish Club with a restaurant and a bar.

1 – Straight Line To Repentance

The club happily welcomed me. This is where I began my daily drinking. Living alone I did what I pleased. I let *le connard* become a more powerful force in my life. I guess I wearied of trying to control him. After all, he was generally right. The drinking quieted the anxiety that was always with me. But I was frequently having flashbacks to when Cheever molested me. I felt like I was present with him. My heart would race, I would start to shake and sweat. I never told anyone about this before but some of those feelings are still present.

With this background anxiety and flashbacks going on in the background, I continued working and living in Salem for the next few months when late in the summer of my 18th year I received a letter from the U.S. Draft Board. My heart was pounding when I opened it. All I could think of was the scene in the movie Alice's Restaurant where Arlo Guthrie is drafted. To avoid going to Viet Nam he switches his urine with someone else's urine during the physical at the induction center. The only question I had was, "Who was I going to get to piss in a cup for me?"

The Korean War had ended in what I understood as a stalemate. Now the U.S. was at war in Viet Nam. Brothers of friends had been sent over there. They often came back messed up one way or another – or not at all. I went to my pediatrician, but he refused to give me a letter asking the draft board to defer me from the draft because of my congenital heart murmur. With no other option, I went to the draft office for advice.

Amend a Broken Mind

Mrs. Fitzgerald was on duty that day. I knew her through my parents. She turned out to be very helpful. When I showed her my draft notice. She smiled and said, "Chad, aren't you going to college?"

I grimaced -- like a child sucking on a lemon. "No," I muttered. "Where would I go?"

She pointed to the local community college located across the street from the draft office. "How about there?" She asked.

I had no idea the place existed, but I left Mrs. Fitzgerald, walked across the street, filled out forms to apply for the fall semester, and paid a $25.00 deposit. Then I returned to the draft office with my enrollment papers. With a smile, Mrs. Fitzgerald stamped my draft card with a 2S. I had just been given a student deferment from the draft; valid as-long-as I stayed in college (or the law changed).

I discovered that college was not at all like high school -- I really enjoyed it. The girls seemed to like me, the teachers treated the students like adults, and I discovered that I could do well academically. For the most part *le connard* quieted down too.

The only negative experience I can remember is the time I went to the career counselling office. When I walked into the office the counsellor was at his desk talking with a pretty, smiling, giggling girl. I waited quietly while they continued to

1 – STRAIGHT LINE TO REPENTANCE

flirt with each other. He finally looked up at me and asked, "What do you want?"

I replied, "I'd like some career counselling."

He said, "What do you want to do?"

I responded, "I don't know."

He rolled his eyes, smirked at the girl and said, "Well then, what do you think I can do for you?"

It took only a second to realize that he was dismissing me. Feeling humiliated, I simply looked at him, turned around, and left his office with the two of them laughing in the background. Experience had taught me that it was a waste of time to try to work with that type of person. I was ready to drop it. However, *le connard* spoke up. He pushed me to act. He even proposed some schemes to get back at him. "Teach him a lesson," *le connard* insisted.

After a week of obsessing over the incident I went to the Dean of Students and said. "I would like some counseling about what I should study."

He replied, "You need to go see the counselor on the first floor."

"I did," I responded. "But he refused to help me. He said there was nothing he could do for me."

Amend a Broken Mind

After a few more questions, he said he would find out what was going on and get back to me. Later that week I heard that the counselor had been fired. I felt a wave of regret. I did not want to hurt the guy. However, apparently, I wasn't the only one the guy had abruptly dismissed.

Le connard rejoiced. "See?" He said to me. "He deserved what he got. You can't continue to let the people in power walk all over you."

"I don't know," I thought. "But I should have gone back and given him another chance."

"Bah," *le connard* replied. "Stop being such a wimp!"

Le connard obviously had better living skills than I. Therefore, I listened to him more and more while trying to maintain the façade of the person I wanted to be.

That autumn a Nor'easter storm was churning up the sea off the coast and the waves banging onto the shore were huge. I had been driving around alone and drinking. Finding myself in Gloucester I parked at Good Harbor beach to watch the waves crash on the beach. *Le connard* convinced me that I should go body surfing even though I was alone, and I knew that there was a strong undertow pulling offshore. "Don't be a wimp," He said." It'll be fun."

I threw my shirt and shoes on the beach and ran into the water with only my shorts on. The water was warm because of the tropical nature of the storm and, without being aware of it,

1 – STRAIGHT LINE TO REPENTANCE

with my back to the shore watching for waves, I was soon washed well offshore. Eventually I got tired and began to develop a chill. I turned to head back to shore but was shocked to see that I was at least one-half of a mile away from the beach. *Le connard* laughed at me and showed me the view from above. "Got ya! How're you gonna get out of this one?"

There were people on the beach waving to get my attention. "Now what do I do?" I said out loud to myself. There was no answer from *le connard* who got me into this mess. However, at that moment I turned back toward the waves and saw a huge roller coming at me. It looked to be 15 feet tall, so I turned around and swam with all I had to match the speed of the wave and ride it in. The wave caught me up, lifted me to the crest as I held my arms out forward and tucked my head between them. I kicked with all my might and the wave carried me toward shore, tugging and shoving me this way and that, while I used all my strength to hold myself straight and keep with the waves forward path.

That ride must have been only seconds long, however, it seemed like a long time before I finally felt myself reach shore. I was manic with adrenaline while I lay in the sand with water around me and the roar of the waves behind me. The people on the beach were yelling obscenities at me and calling me names but all I could hear was *le connard* laughing, He said, "I told you it would be the coolest thing you ever did."

Amend a Broken Mind

I laughed out loud and could not stop grinning. He was right! "I did it and lived to tell about it," I thought as I exhaustedly shuffled up the beach.

"Now", *le connard* said, "More beer!"

The adrenalin was still flooding my system and a few more beers got me very manic and not a little drunk. My resistance to *le connard's* influence was always lower when I drank alcohol. So, when, suddenly, on the way along the coast road with Good Harbor in the mist behind me, *le connard* shouted, "You need to stop. Now!"

I did what he said and stopped the car on a side street, got out and began walking through the yards of the homes in the neighborhood. I came up to a big four-square home and he said, "Up the gutter!"

Not thinking at all about the consequences, I began climbing. I had so much adrenaline I scampered right up to a second story porch. I looked inside and heard voices coming from downstairs – a shower was running in the bathroom to my left. Then I heard the phone ring downstairs. Someone answered and said, "What? Someone's on the upstairs porch?"

Le connard laughed, and I scrambled back down and walked quickly back to my car. As I left the neighborhood, I saw the police pull up to the house I had just left. Again, the adrenalin was flowing, and I laughed along with *le connard* as I drove away.

1 – STRAIGHT LINE TO REPENTANCE

As time passed, I began to have panic attacks and I was afraid to be alone. I was constantly frightened. To even sit down and be alone in my room and have my body be floating around me, imagine that! It was terrifying. I was utterly petrified that somebody might find out what was really going on inside of me.

AMEND A BROKEN MIND

2 – UNEXPECTED CHANGE IN DIRECTION

Somewhere along the line, I discovered that working towards a goal helped a whole lot to keep the anxiety away. Accordingly, I made getting a college degree a goal. As classes started, I became immersed in the work of studying and doing the work the professors assigned. In between classes I hung out in the cafeteria with a bunch of girls with whom I enjoyed flirting. I had signed up for an Associates of Arts program with the thought of transferring to a four-year college eventually. This program required me to take a foreign language. I chose French. As such, one morning I was studying for a French exam at the back of the cafeteria away from the regular crowd when a young woman I never saw before sat across the table from me. I ignored her.

She said, "Are you studying French?"

I did not look up but continued to try to study only grunting in reply.

She did not give up easily, "Who do you have?"

I mumbled without looking up, "Cote'." And continued trying to study.

Then she said with a smile in her voice," Oh, I have Cote' too."

2 – UNEXPECTED CHANGE IN DIRECTION

Exasperated, I looked up with the intention of asking her to go away. However, what I saw totally made me forget French, Cote' and the upcoming exam. Standing before me was the most beautiful young woman I had seen at the school. She was about 5' 3" with long blond hair and curves in all the right places. I put down my French book and smiled. Her name was Sharon and soon she had me comfortable enough to confess that I was not doing well in French. I never picked up the study habit in high school and I was struggling with the classes that required studying. She offered to help me after school, and I walked her to her next class. We cut classes the next day and went to the Cranes Beach where I pushed her down a sand dune and kissed her.

The next few years were spent going to classes and spending time with Sharon. We did all sorts of different things. During most of them I endeavored to better understand Sharon's personality. To illustrate I give the following example. I had an 18-foot O'Day day sailor sailboat. It was moored in Salem Harbor. Long before I met Sharon, I had learned the value of taking people out for a sail in any sailboat that had no auxiliary power other than a canoe paddle or pair of oars. Without a motor onboard, a sailing trip with me could last one hour or ten hours – depending on the weather. When I was younger, I would take my sisters out and learned that only Debbie had the personality that would not only let her "go with the flow" of events as they occurred but would let her actually enjoy the

Amend a Broken Mind

challenge of the unknown. My other sisters were either terrified or bored.

Later, when I was in high school, I met a kid who I got friendly with and I wanted to know if I could trust him. I took him out on my boat at the time, a handmade 18-foot sloop, with the idea that we would go to Misery Island to explore. Misery Island lies in Beverly harbor and is a few miles as the crow flies from Salem Harbor and my boat mooring. There was very little wind that day and, instead of just enjoying the time together, he began obsessing with the time it was taking to reach our destination. He could see the island ahead, due North and tantalizingly near but there was little wind and we were just ghosting along with the currents and tides – making very little headway. He finally could not take any more and started paddling with the canoe oar that I had on board for emergencies.

We were making slow but steady progress when the wind began to pick-up. Unfortunately, it came directly from the North which was where we wanted to go. I began to tack the boat so that we could zig zag our way forward into the face of the wind. However, my friend had had enough. He started swearing at me and shaking the oar at me. He loudly demanded, "Stop messing with me!"

I tried to calmly explain to him what I was doing, how the process of tacking the boat would get us there eventually. However, he began to slam the oar handle on the gunwale

2 – Unexpected Change in Direction

cursing me, the wind and the boat until the oar broke in half. He then tossed the pieces of the broken oar overboard with a loud, "That is what I think of you and your damn boat."

I could not watch his antics anymore (I was angry about the oar too), so I came about and, with the wind at our backs, headed back to Salem Harbor and the mooring. At this, my friend was even more frustrated. Misery Island was only a hundred yards away when I began to head back, and he could see the island slipping away. There is nowhere to hide on a 12-foot boat, but he went as far forward as he could while I remained in the stern with the rudder and the sheets. We returned to the mooring in silence and, after making the boat fast, I drove him home. I never saw him again.

Sharon, however, was so comfortable on the boat and with me that we spent hours sailing along in good wind, drifting when there was no wind, and exploring the islands. One time we found ourselves hanging on for dear life when a Coast Guard Sikorsky S-16R (HH-3F Pelican) helicopter lifted off from the Salem Coast Guard Station and flew right over us at about 50 feet causing my 18 foot day sailor to go right up on beams end. She laughed along with me as we sat on the gunwale with the tip of the mast almost touching the water from the force of the prop down wash.

We climbed Mount Washington in the early spring with skis and overnight gear. Only to find out after a day of skiing on the 20-foot snow base at the Head Wall that we could not set-up our

Amend a Broken Mind

tent and spend the night in Tuckerman's Ravine without a reservation. She gamely hiked back down with me and we set-up my two-man pup tent next the Swift River along the Kancamagus Highway in Conway, New Hampshire. Sharon was always a good sport during our adventures seeming to just enjoy our time together.

Now that I had school, a job and Sharon in my life *Le connard's* influence waned and he became less of a driving factor. I threw myself into the schoolwork and spent all my free time with Sharon. My anxiety even became more manageable. However, I still drank. I asked Sharon to marry me a few years later when it became clear to me that she was good for me and we got along very well. Her response was, "Ask me when you are sober."

I did ask her again when I was sober. We got married six months later in August of 1974. One week later while we were on our honeymoon, we left a rum swizzle party to go back to our room to watch President Nixon resign on TV. When we returned from our honeymoon at the Reefs we settled into an apartment in Sharon's hometown and she finished her two-year degree at the community college while working at the local YMCA. I took a part time job at a grocery store and attended college full time. Eventually I graduated with a Baccalaureate degree and looked toward graduate school. Sharon wanted to start having kids. So, we compromised. I went out and got a full-time job and she got pregnant.

2 – Unexpected Change in Direction

We have two children from those years. The oldest is a boy we named Sean born 1976. Then came Kate in 1979. Sean was a tow-headed bundle of joy. Sharon was gaga over him. During the pre-birth period we went to parenting classes and I was told that it was not unusual for the first-time father to be jealous of the newborn child. I shrugged that off as being childish.

I guess that means that I was childish, because I was very jealous of our newborn son when he arrived. I would come home from work and listen to Sharon tell me about how Sean did this, and Sean did that. I mean, according to her Sean's poop didn't stink. I remember thinking, "How about asking me, how was your day, honey?"

It was during this time that my drinking increased, and *le connard* became more vocal than he was in our earlier marriage.

Eventually, as our family grew, we bought a house in a small town 20-minutes North of the home in which I grew up. At the time, the town had a population of 3,400 people, a dozen small farms, open land, a small downtown area and an X-rated drive-in movie theater over near the interstate. The house was a real fixer-upper and far enough away from Boston that house prices were still reasonable. I remember thinking, "We are the only people in town without a pickup truck."

Now, 40 years later, we have rebuilt the house from inside out. The character of the town has changed. Most of the farms have been turned into subdivision of million-dollar homes. My

Amend a Broken Mind

joke now is that we are the only people without a Mercedes Benz.

As I look back to those days, I realize that I worked hard to maintain a façade on the outside of a respectable father and husband. However, as the stresses of being the sole provider for a growing family increased the influence of *le connard* also grew. I began drinking daily – a habit I got out of when we were first married. Now, however, I schemed to hide my drinking. After work I would go out to the garage with the pretense of fixing something. It was in the garage that I hid my booze. After a few drinks I would find an excuse to go off in the car to drive around, drink and try to escape the growing anxiety. *Le connard* would fill my mind with anxiety, fears, doubts and insecurities.

I developed a conviction that I was not qualified for the work that I was doing. My first job out of college was with a large multinational company working as an industrial microbiologist in their Microbiology Lab. Part of my job was to test the ability of different chemical compounds to kill microbes and fungi. I would formulate the compounds into vinyl film and place them outside on racks to expose the plastic to the environment and evaluate them for microbial susceptibility.

I enjoyed lab work. It was repetitive and physical (except when I had to write reports). My efforts screening chemicals for anti-microbial activity eventually resulted in a report where I identified a compound that killed bacteria and fungi but was not toxic to humans. It found immediate application in adult diapers

2 – UNEXPECTED CHANGE IN DIRECTION

and bed clothes. Sales began to rise. I was promoted to marketing where I traveled with the salespeople explaining to prospective customers the benefits of our new product. Notwithstanding the success I was experiencing, I was consumed by a nagging feeling of inadequacy.

I did enjoy the travel and meeting people and, as it turned out, I was good at talking with customers on a technical level. However, my expense account included an entertainment section and all the alcohol I could drink. I used the alcohol to bolster my confidence. Finding that as time went on, I needed more and more liquor to do the job – to quell the anxieties.

My drinking and drunkenness became more frequent and my behavior became more out of control. One day in the summer of 1980, I was invited to play in a golf tournament with the product manager and a customer at a local club. My foursome won the tournament and we gathered at the clubhouse for drinks. After a few drinks with my teammates, I left because I did not want them to see me drunk and I wanted to drink more.

Later that night I went into a stranger's house, with *le connard's* encouragement, as I had done without incident that time after my escape from drowning. However, an earlier folly does not justify a later one and this time I was confronted by a woman who saw me hiding in a cupboard. I left quickly and she called the local police. They picked me up a little later and I was arrested. I spent the night in the police station jail to be arraigned the next morning.

Amend a Broken Mind

At the courthouse I pleaded not guilty and was released on $100,000.00 bail that my parents put up. I was overwhelmed with shame. The next day, at my parent's home I was crying and confused about what had happened the night before. I never thought about what would happen if I got caught. My mother asked, "Chad, do you need some help?"

I replied, "Yes! I don't understand what is going on in my mind."

I think, in retrospect, that when we elect to take a certain path, be it folly or not, some avenues close off right away while, at the same time, others open with opportunity. I do not know, of course, what my life would have been like if I had not decided to walk into that stranger's house on that evening at that time. However, I have since recognized that the avenue that opened for me that evening was to define the rest of my life.

The avenue that opened came in the guise of a mental health counselor in a local town. My mother had heard good things about him. I called and made an appointment. His name was Dr. Stone. When the day came to meet him, I took time off from work and drove to his office. My heart was beating like crazy and my level of anxiety was high. At this point, the people in my office knew nothing about what had happened to me and *le connard* was working on me to forget about going to the shrink. He encouraged me to submit to the compulsion to go out and get drunk.

2 – UNEXPECTED CHANGE IN DIRECTION

However, I was determined to act in a positive way and headed to my appointment. Along with the voice of *le connard,* my thoughts were racing with confusion and the fear that I was crazy. In fact, for years I thought of my existence as walking on a tight rope between sanity and insanity – just waiting for a push or stumble leading me to fall one way or the other. As I drove to the psychiatrist's office that beautiful summer morning in my 28th year struggling against the desire to scream frig-it and get drunk, I felt like I had fallen off the tight rope into insanity.

After my arrest, somewhere in my chaotic thinking, I recalled the words of a contributor to a book I had read titled "Don't Call Me Crazy". As I recall, the contributor realized that there were things about herself that she could not change no matter what she did or how much she wanted the change. She questioned the idea of free will because of the obsessions that resisted every effort she made to gain control over herself and how she was unable to be the kind of person she wanted to be. She also realized that external forces acting on her life were often outside of her internal control. Lack of internal control led to a feeling of helplessness and helplessness led to a feeling of hopelessness and hopelessness led to despair.

Accordingly, I have come to believe that it is not always our intentions or our decisions that guide and shape our lives. More often than we want to accept, impulse creates our tale. Furthermore, what we remember of our own tale can be inaccurate. Beyond this, we are often carried by the events of our time. We might fly where we would like but our arrival is out of our control. We might decide college is not for us until we get drafted for a war on the other side of the world and we avoid participating in that war by attending college. Our own plans, timetables with arrivals and departure times, allow an illusion of command. But it is only an illusion.

While *le connard* encouraged self-destructive behavior, following his instructions gave me a feeling of power. However, after I acted on *le connard's* directives I was often overwhelmed with shame and regret. A period followed where I was hyper focused on my behavior towards others and on my appearance. I also became hyper helpful to those around me. I was trying to gain control over the compulsions but, like waves breaking on the shore, I was caught in a cycle. Each stage in this cycle passed moving onto the next. Hopelessness became a dark and frequent companion. I began to think continuously about ending my life.

On the North bound side of the local highway there existed a small rest area on the right just before the bridge that spanned the Merrimac River. The parking area of this rest stop has since been closed. However, at the time it led to a cliff that dropped about 100 feet to the river below. Overwhelmed with hopelessness, I would head up the highway in my car at high speed and enter the rest area toward the cliff only to chicken out at the last minute and pound on the brake. Then I would sit in the car, surrounded by dust, heart pounding, the sound of

2 – UNEXPECTED CHANGE IN DIRECTION

squealing breaks and the ticking of the stalled engine ringing in my ears. I looked over at the river and wept.

In the psychiatrist's office, Dr. Stone asked me what my complaint was, and I told him, "I think I'm going crazy,"

We talked about the night of my arrest. He asked, "Do you drink or do drugs?"

I told him, "I drink a little bit every day."

He then asked me a series of questions, "Do you hide your drinking? Does your drinking affect your job and relationships? Do you find yourself unable to stop drinking even though you really want to? Do you do things while drinking that you regret afterwards?"

My answers, "Yes, yes, yes, yes."

And he said, "I think you might have a problem with alcohol."

Dr. Stone suggested I go to a detoxification hospital. He recommended one in New Hampshire. "It will look good to the judge," he said.

I went to the hospital as suggested and they put me into a locked ward after removing everything I had. They dressed me in sweatpants and a t-shirt that they provided. During the first week I attended an Alcoholics Anonymous meeting. At this meeting I found myself thinking, "I identify with what the speaker is saying."

Amend a Broken Mind

One speaker emphasized how important it was to, "Do the 12 steps."

When I got back to my bunk after that first meeting, I opened the big book of AA that they gave me and found the pages containing the twelve steps. I read through them. The first step was, "Admit that we have a problem with alcohol, and we are powerless to stop drinking."

"No problem there," I reflected. "Why else would I be where I am right now? I have no power, the staff of the hospital tells me when to eat, sleep, come and go. Now that is powerlessness."

The second step was, "Came to believe that a power greater than myself could restore me to sanity." I thought, "There has been no evidence of a higher power in my life except for the Commonwealth of Massachusetts which arrested me. So, we will see what happens there."

The third step, "Turned our will and our life over to that higher power". With the trial facing burglary charges coming up and not knowing what that meant for my future I felt very powerless and had to turn things over to the state and my lawyer. So, I checked that step off as completed.

I went through the rest of the steps and made a cursory stab at each one. When I had finished, I shut the book with the realization that alcohol was at least one of my problems. I must laugh at myself now as I write this. The steps of Alcoholics

2 – Unexpected Change in Direction

Anonymous are part of a continuous program that takes a lifetime to complete and regular repetition to keep from back sliding. However, I was at least willing to try and that was the beginning of the road of recovery for me.

Amend a Broken Mind

3 – Into the Pit

My trial was short. I pleaded guilty to burglary. Although, I didn't understand what that really meant. My lawyer said that was what I should do -- so I did what he said. He told me that I had no record and they would probably sentence me to probation. The prosecuting attorney told the judge that I was a danger to society. My attorney told the judge that I was a "good guy", that I was a family man, that I owned a home, that I was fully employed, and I that I had no previous offenses on record.

The judge listened to both sides then banged his gavel and said, "10 years for burglary."

There was a moment of stunned silence broken by my wife screaming. The court officer rushed over to her and began to pull her from the court room. I looked over and saw my mother hitting the officer over the head with her pocketbook yelling, "Leave her alone!"

While this was going on, another court officer approached me, put hand cuffs and shackles on me, and led me from the court room. I was held in a locked room at the courthouse until session was over. Then I was put in the back of a Sheriff's van with the other convicts of the day. We were all taken to the state's medium security prison in Concord, Massachusetts. At the prison intake room, I was told by a prison officer to strip. The officer searched me thoroughly – a finger in the rectum, a glance down the throat. He took my clothes and gave me some

3 – INTO THE PIT

oversized jeans and a t-shirt. I signed a voucher for my things and, once dressed, I was taken to the New-Line where I was placed in a cell with three other men. One of the men asked me what I was in for and I replied, "Burglary."

He asked, "Was it a good one?"

I responded, "Not really. I'm in here aren't I?"

The opening to the cell was a sliding, bared door. It looked out onto a catwalk that went by my cell and around the perimeter of a long, rectangular, three-story, open room. Guards walked the catwalk, looking into the open, barred cells. There were dozens of cells on the long sides. I was on the third floor and, if I stood on my tiptoes on one of the bunks, I could see down the opening in the middle to a courtyard three floors below. In the courtyard were metal tables and chairs bolted to the floor.

The design of this building enhanced the sound in an echoey way creating a constant drone. A cacophony blended from three open floors holding hundreds of men, arguing, banging the bars, yelling, muttering and cursing everything and everyone. Every now and then the noise was punctuated by the loud slamming of steel doors.

Sometime before the trial I ceased hearing from *le connard*. It was as if he had cajoled me into behaving a certain way then disappeared when the consequences were due. I was extremely disappointed in myself. At the same time, the control *le connard*

AMEND A BROKEN MIND

had gained over my personality had been almost complete: he powerfully helped me justify my drinking; he thrilled over the rush of adrenalin that flooded me when I took risks; and he helped me hide the duality to everyone around me. Now that he was gone, I felt a freedom that had been missing for a long time. At the same time, however, I felt exposed – oddly terribly alone.

There was plenty of time while sitting in the cell to dwell on or brood over the course of the ethical deterioration that I experienced over the years. Time to remember the continuous pushing of the limits. I kept asking myself when it started? When did *le connard* first make his vile appearance? The Catholic doctrine I learned as a child seemed to confirm the idea that we have a sinful nature that is constantly in conflict with God's grace. But, what role did alcohol play in all this? Did the lead and mercury poisoning I got when I was a child contribute to the path I took? I tried to understand but I had a lot of unanswered questions.

After two weeks on the New-Line, I was released to Population where I shared a room with one other inmate. Population consisted of a cluster of low, identical, single-story buildings. Inside each was a corridor down the center. Cells, with two cons (jail-house slang for inmate) in each, lined either side of the corridor. The screws (jail-house slang for guards) let us cons out for breakfast, lunch, yard-time and dinner. To get out of my cell more often, I got a job washing and waxing the floors in different parts of the joint.

3 – INTO THE PIT

My favorite floor to wash was the one in the main guard tower. I liked it because I was usually alone up there. From the tower I could see the traffic going by on the old Mohawk Trail. I watched longingly. The view showed a bit of normal life in my otherwise abnormal day. I would light a cigarette and watch the traffic go by until one of the guards down below yelled my name and I had to come down.

The man I shared a cell with told me that he recently was picked up after having escaped. He was a big white guy with a constant scowl on his face and an obsessive personality.

"I was this close to that bitch of an ex-wife," he growled while holding his thumb and index finger slightly apart. "But the bastards caught up to me before I could kill the bitch."

When he busted out, he told me, his objective was to kill his ex-wife. He got to within 50 feet of her before the authorities grabbed him. He said, "I'm going to kill that bitch someday. I don't care how long it takes."

I responded, "Maybe you should just forget her."

He looked at me, his face screwed up with anger, vein bulging on his neck, and said, "Maybe I should kill you instead."

The cell was only ten feet by eight feet with bunk beds against one wall and a toilet and sink on the opposite wall. It was less noisy than the open arrangement in the new line because the doors were solid with one small unbreakable

Amend a Broken Mind

window for the guards to peek at us during a count. As is was, I had nowhere to go to get away from him.

I did not sleep well that night. My cellmate was in the bunk below me and his threat still rang in my ears. Also, it was August and very hot and humid. That night I was laying on my back on the top bunk with a bed sheet at my feet when I felt something drop onto and crawl around on my chest. I grabbed at it and then there was another, and another. I grabbed one and held it up squirming in the weak light. It was a cockroach. They were falling from the ceiling onto my chest! I wiped them off me with my hand and pulled the sheet over my body. I eventually dropped off to sleep from exhaustion.

The next day, while I was working in the visiting room, my cellmate was moved to a maximum-security prison on the other side of the state. After lunch I sat on the lower bunk and enjoyed the time alone. One month had passed since the trial. Later that day the solid door of the cell slid open quite suddenly and two officers stood aside and pushed a teen age boy into my cell.

His name was Rickie and he was crying. He told me that he was high on crack one night when he decided he needed some whiskey and walked into a package store carrying a shotgun. While in the package-store he began to shoot at the bottles behind the counter. He tearfully told me that he was convicted of armed robbery and attempted murder. He kept repeating, in

3 – INTO THE PIT

tears, that he was ashamed of himself and, "What must my mother think of me?"

I suggested he write to her and tell her what he told me. He said between sobs, "But, I can't write. I can't read or write."

I offered to write a letter for him while he dictated. When we finished with the letter, I began to teach him the alphabet. He was a quick learner and it was not long before he was able to write simple letters to his mother. It also kept me busy and helped keep my mind away from negative thoughts.

I mentioned earlier that we were let out to the yard for an hour each day. The first time I went out to the yard for recreation I was approached by someone wanting to bum a cigarette. When I said no, he pulled a homemade shank from his pocket. I gave him the pack. Then another con approached me and offered to sell me weed. After that I began running around the perimeter of the yard just to keep everyone away from me. Five laps equaled one mile. Around and around I ran each day. While I was running no one bothered me.

When the weather was bad, I hung out in the weight room and began to develop an exercise routine. My body began to respond to the regimen, and I started gaining weight. During this period, one of the Hispanic guys asked me if I would get into the boxing ring and spar with him. I did and over the winter I started boxing regularly. I learned some things about myself that I did not know and discovered I could hold my own in the ring. My self-confidence grew.

AMEND A BROKEN MIND

I also attended Alcoholics Anonymous meetings and church services. When I got to the prison, I heard that people from AA would come into the joint from the outside once a week and share their experience, strength and hope with the inmates. I found that I identified with the experiences they shared and particularly remember the first time I heard the promises read. They are in the big book of Alcohol Anonymous and go like this:

> *We are going to know a new freedom and a new happiness. We will not regret the past nor wish to shut the door on it. We will comprehend the word "serenity" and we will know peace. No matter how far down the scale we have gone we will see how our experience can benefit others. The feeling of uselessness and self-pity will disappear. We will lose interest in selfish things and gain interest in our fellows. Self-seeking will slip away. Our whole attitude and outlook upon life will change. Fear of people and or economic insecurity will leave us. We will intuitively know how to handle situations which used to baffle us. We will suddenly realize that God is doing for us what we could not do for ourselves.* [1]

I wanted all those things in my life. So, I kept going to meetings. Besides, what they said in the meetings was true, "It was better than hanging out in my cell."

As I related earlier, I was raised Catholic but did not really believe in God. However, I wanted more reasons to get out of

3 – INTO THE PIT

my cell, so I started attending Catholic services. The priest was a young man who was uncomfortable being in the prison with us cons. One day he was talking about us all being sinners including himself. One of the other convicts, a large muscular man who had been in prison for ten years and lifted weights every day, stood up, put his hands on his hips and confronted him, "What could you have done that was so bad, Father?"

The priest turned red, mumbled something and changed the subject.

That priest never returned so I started going to the Protestant services. When I first visited with Pastor Tomlin I told him I thought I was an alcoholic and had been without a drink for four months. He asked me how I felt. I said, "I feel like I've been born again."

He replied as any good evangelical would. With a big smile he asked, "Oh, have you seen Jesus?"

I was a little taken aback with his question because that is not what I meant. However, I answered him, albeit shyly, "I don't think so."

He must have realized his mistake, but he did not push the issue. I started attending his services regularly and took part where I could. Again, mainly because it got me out of my cell. There was another reason though. Many of the men I saw every day were very sick and confused in their minds. Pastor Tomlin was a sane person with whom I could have a normal conversation. Every con I spoke to was either scheming to take advantage of someone in the jail, planning to get back at someone who was responsible for getting them in prison, or suffering from mental illness.

For example, there was a young man in the cell across the aisle from me who was so depressed that he did not leave his bunk -- ever. His cellmate brought him food every day, but the guy never moved from his bunk. I looked in one day and spoke to him. He did not respond or even look at me, so I left him alone. In the cell next to mine was a Vietnam veteran who was in jail for drug violations. He spent his time making booze in his cell until the guards found out and raided his cell. He was immediately transported to the maximum-security prison at Walpole. Another man spent his days walking up and down the corridor repeatedly muttering over and over, "I gotta get outta here!"

Then there was the convict who had found Buddha and spent his time meditating in the lotus position. Yet another worshiped a demon and spent his time writing odd symbols in a notebook. The notebook was a few hundred pages thick and filled with extremely neat but unintelligible pencil script. When I asked what the symbols meant he looked me right in the eye and said, "I don't know what they mean but I am told by Satan to write them down."

3 – INTO THE PIT

Another con came into my cell one day as I was leaving for my job and asked to bum a cigarette. I said, "No. I only have two left."

He pulled a shank out of his pocket, held it to my neck, and said, "You will give them to me."

This was the second time this had happened over cigarettes. I quit smoking that day for good.

My biggest emotional issue at the time was shame. I had not heard from *le connard* since I walked through the doors of the prison. However, after three months at Concord in the Massachusetts Correctional Center I was transported in handcuffs and shackles to Shirley Prison. I was three months into a ten-year felony burglary sentence.

That morning I had no idea that I was going to be moved (or lugged as the slang calls it) to another joint. I was in a welding class when my cellmate Rickie burst in to tell me that I was wanted at the prison front office. I put my welding tools away and asked Rickie, "What's going on?"

He was unusually tight lipped and just answered, "Come on. You're wasting time."

We hurried across the field towards the main office with me asking questions and Rickie limiting his responses to, "Come on. Come on. You're moving too slow."

Amend a Broken Mind

He had a big shit eating grin on his face, and I could not figure out what was up. However, when we arrived at the main office, he shook my hand, gave me a hug, and said, "I'll write to you."

Rickie turned and left while the guards put shackles and hand cuffs on me. The guards then led me to a Sheriff's van, helped me inside, and tossed in a box containing my clothes and other personal stuff without saying a word about what was going on or where I was going. I thought to myself, "I am being lugged to the maximum-security prison at Walpole, Massachusetts. But, why was Rickie grinning like he was when he said goodbye?"

When we drove through the gate at Shirley Prison, I was relieved. According to prisoner scuttlebutt, this meant that I would soon be eligible to meet with the parole board. I experienced a faint feeling of hope. However, I soon found out that although the security was at level lower than it was at Concord the population was still made up of the same group of people. Consequently, my life was threatened twice in my first couple of days there.

During the intake interview I told the intake officer that I had a problem with alcohol. He sent me to meet with the Alcoholics Anonymous Coordinator Dick McCallum. Dick was seated at a metal, state-issue desk in a small office in the prison administration building and was expecting me. He told me to sit down and asked me to tell my story. I told him the whole story:

3 – INTO THE PIT

how I had been drinking and walked into a stranger's house; how the occupant called the police and how I was arrested; I told him about my 30-days in a detox; and finally how I was sentenced to 10-years for burglary. In conclusion I said, "I'm an idiot and ashamed of myself."

Dick's own story was remarkable. By his own admission, he was a drunk, although a sober one. When he was younger, he would drink every day to oblivion. His behavior was totally out of control. He often had black-outs and would wake-up in a jail cell. One morning he found himself in the local jail with no idea how he got there. He called the jailer to let him out as they usually did in the morning. But this time he was told he was not going anywhere. The previous evening, he was told, he had killed a police officer and he would not be getting out for a very long time.

He was eventually convicted of second-degree murder and received a life sentence. In prison he was so out of control and self-destructive that he was sent to Bridgewater State Mental Hospital where he was kept in a padded cell. The door to his padded room was a hatch door in the ceiling. He told me how he would spend his days screaming -- throwing his food and feces at the walls and guards.

One day, as he sat in his own filth in his hole, a preacher stopped by to see him.

"Richard McCallum are you in there?" the preacher called from above.

Amend a Broken Mind

Dick's hollow response came slowly from below, "Leave me alone."

The preacher replied, "Your mother asked me to come by and pray for you."

Dick was quiet. He did not respond until the preacher said, "Do you know how much you have hurt your mother?"

Dick told me that he was so overcome by the thought of his mother that he broke down and began to weep uncontrollably. He did not remember the preacher praying for him but before he left, the man tossed a Bible down to Dick. Dick eventually regained control of himself. He started to read the Bible that the pastor had left behind.

Years later, a completely changed man, he received a pardon from the Governor of the Commonwealth. When I met Dick, he ran the drug and alcohol treatment program at Shirley. We talked frequently while I was there. I did not trust him when I first met him. He wore a dark blue knit cap on his bald head; tan, cotton slacks; a plaid, collared shirt unbuttoned at the neck; and running sneakers. His face was lumpy and scarred from many beatings. His nose obviously had been broken more than once. Cauliflower ears and one glass eye completed the picture -- not the kind of face one saw in the neighborhood in which I was raised.

It was either the second or third meeting that I told him that one of the inmates threatened to stick me with his homemade

3 – INTO THE PIT

knife. I didn't expect the response I got from Dick. He took his glass eye out of the socket and put it on the table in front of me. With a big grin he said, "Don't worry Chad." Pointing to the glass eyeball on the table he went on, "This eye will always be looking out for you."

At that he laughed deep and hearty as he repeatedly removed and replaced knit cap that he always wore on his bald head. Then he told me to go back to my cell, get down on my knees, and asked God to help me. I replied, "Come on Dick, there is no God."

He replied, "Do you trust me? "

By this time, we had shared enough with each other that I had come to grudgingly trust him, so I nodded, and he continued," Then do it because I believe. Let's see what happens."

When I got back to my cell, I did what Dick told me to do. I felt like a weirdo and could not kneel by my bed. But I lay down and said quietly, lest someone overhear, "God, if you are there please help me. Dick says you will so please help me know what to do."

Later that night the con who threatened me was lugged to Walpole.

During another meeting Dick said to me, "The doctors are amazed that I am still living because my heart is so bad. Only 20% of it is functioning."

Amend a Broken Mind

Then he said, "But, you know Chad." He paused for effect, "God is keeping me alive long enough to see you get sober."

That really moved me. Dick's simple statement was full of an unconditional love – something I had not identified before. I was also moved considerably by a letter written in Rickie's handwriting that was delivered to me. It was simple and childlike, but it was a great encouragement.

After a while at Shirley I was notified that I would go before the parole board. I remember very little of what went on during that hearing (I was very nervous). What I do remember is entering a room and standing before a table behind which sat two women and a man with very stern expressions. After looking into my record and asking a few questions, they decided I would be released on parole at the end of my first year in the joint. There were two main conditions to my release -- I must find a job before they would let me go and I must continue attending Alcoholics Anonymous meetings. By this time, I had no problem admitting I had a problem with booze and that my life was unmanageable (the first step in AA). In my mind it was a sure thing that my arrest was at least partly the result of that last day of drinking. It was also a sure thing that my life was unmanageable. Afterall, in prison I was told what to wear, when to eat, when to go out, when to come in, etc.

By the time I appeared before the parole board, I had been sober for 12-months and I was full of anxiety about how I was going to keep from drinking out in the real world. I also had to

3 – INTO THE PIT

find a job before I would be released. I talked to Dick about these two concerns. He said, "I can help you with a contact in AA on the outside. But I suggest you get down on your knees and ask God about the job."

Instead of doing what Dick said, I sent out a bunch of resumes to technology companies. I used my parent's address and my mother told me about the responses I received. I had a good-looking resume (strategically leaving out the jail portion) and the responses started coming in. One company, Digital Equipment Corporation, asked me to come in for an interview. My mother brought me a suit and tie and took me to the interview.

It was a beautiful New England spring day – cool and sunny. The spring leaves budding bright green on the trees seemed to indicate renewal. I was feeling positive, relaxed, and confident. We pulled into the Digital campus with the professionally landscaped grounds and modern buildings. I thought, "I can see myself working here. This will be good."

The interview went well. The position was for an inside salesperson. I spoke with the personnel manager, the sales manager and a couple other salespeople. After a few hours the sales manager, in the presence of the personnel manager, asked me when I could start.

I responded with an innocent smile, "I can start next week. But there is something I must tell you. I am an inmate at MCI

Amend a Broken Mind

Shirley, and I will be commuting from there to the job for a few weeks until my prole period begins."

It was required of me that I say this last statement. And I did say it. I said it word for word from one of the conditions on the parole papers.

The sales manager looked at me, furrowed his brow, and asked, "What's an MCI Shirley?"

I responded confidently and as lightly as I could to assure them that it was of no significant importance, "It's a prison and I am in inmate there."

They looked at each other and the personnel manager said to me, "Excuse us for a minute."

They both got up and left the room. A little while later the personnel manager came back alone and said, "We'll let you know." And I was escorted from the building.

This little scenario played itself out two more times with minor variation before I realized that I was not going to succeed the way I was going at this. I went back to Dick McCallum and told him what happened. He smiled and said, "Did you ask God to help you find work?"

I swear to you, that was all he said. His ugly, grinning face really pissed me off and I annoyingly replied, "Come on Dick. Is that all you have for me?"

3 – INTO THE PIT

He replied, "Do you trust me? Just ask for help and see what happens. What have you got to lose?"

I must confess, I was feeling very hopeless as I walked back to my cell. However, I did as Dick told me and prayed, "God, I don't really believe that this will help but I trust Dick and, well, can you please help me find a job, so I can get out of here?"

When I finished, I sat up and sheepishly looked around just to make sure no one saw me.

A couple days later I was picking up my mail and there was a letter from my youngest sister, Lizzy. It was a nice, newsy letter and I read it through feeling a little wistful. Toward the end she said, "I heard you were looking for work and felt like I should send this job advertisement to you."

Attached to the letter was a notice clipped from a New Hampshire newspaper advertising the position of bricker (mason) at a company located in the town of Billerica. She did not explain why she thought I was qualified for this job. After all, I was not a mason and had never bricked a thing in my life. Furthermore, I was not a very handy person, but, with a shrug, I sent my resume with the advertisement attached to the company in Billerica. Besides, the thought of being a "bricka in Billerica" amused me.

The following week my mother told me the company in Billerica wanted to see me, so I put on my suit and drove to the address in the ad. By this time, I had permission to have a car

Amend a Broken Mind

on the prison premises, so I did not need to put my mother though the process of waiting for hours only to have me rejected again.

This company was a little different from what I was used to. They manufactured high temperature kilns for packaging and materials processing. There was no landscaping and the building was a basic manufacturing structure with office space in front. I was welcomed by the personnel manager and led to a meeting room. Her first question to me was, "Why are you applying for a job as a bricker with a resume like this?"

I just came right out and told her that I was a convicted felon. I was living at MCI Shirley and that I could not get out on parole until I found a job. I told her about my other interviews and that they had all fallen through as soon as I told them about my living arrangements.

She looked at me and said, "We have an opening in sales. Would you be interested in that?"

I was dumbfounded and began to weep. I replied softly, "Yes, please."

She excused herself and came back with the sales manager. He interviewed me and said they had already offered the job to another candidate but, they would keep me in mind. I thanked them and left expecting that I would never hear from them.

3 – INTO THE PIT

A couple days later I got word from the personnel lady that they wanted to offer me the job. When I told Dick McCallum he laughed and said, "What did I tell ya?"

For the next three months I commuted from the prison to the job. When my release date finally arrived, I was released from Shirley at 12:01 am August 18, 1981. I turned 30 during my incarceration and was ready to embark on a new life. Although none of what happened had ever been part of my wildest dreams, I felt grateful and happy. I drove home and when I pulled into the driveway, I saw yellow ribbons tied around the tree in the front yard. It was 1 am when I crawled into bed next to my wife Sharon for the first time in a year.

The next morning, I was sitting in the kitchen when my five-year-old son Sean walked in. He looked at me, hesitated, and said, "What are you doing here?"

Amend a Broken Mind

4 – Revelation

As I write this, I find myself wondering why Sharon did not leave me during those first years of our marriage. Her mother told her that I was the type of guy who would always end up on my feet. However, I asked Sharon once why she stuck around through that period. She simply answered, "Because I love you." That sounded an awful lot like unconditional love, and before Dick entered my life, I did not realize that kind of love existed. However, after forty-five years of marriage to Sharon I now really do understand what unconditional love is. It is like God's love – undeserved but given freely to us non-the-less.

Pastor Tomlin had instilled in me the habit of reading the Bible (even though I stubbornly refused to surrender to belief), and Dick got me into the habit of praying constantly to God for guidance. While I was in prison Sharon started attending a weekly Bible study in a neighbor's home. It seemed that God was working in both our lives.

In 1981, when I got out on parole, I continued to work at the inside sales job and commuted daily home instead of to the joint. However, I was terrified that I would start drinking again and slip into my old habits. Dick McCallum was true to his word. He introduced me to Kevin, a sober alcoholic in the town next to the one I lived in with my family. I got active in Alcoholics Anonymous by going to meetings with Kevin and by sharing my story at jails, hospitals, and detox facilities. The first time I shared my story at an AA meeting, Kevin and I drove to Leominster, Massachusetts. On the way there he said I was going to speak at the meeting. I asked, "How big a group will it be."

He smiled and replied, "Oh, it's a small hall in a church basement."

Eventually, we pulled into the parking lot of a huge Catholic cathedral. In the basement was a large hall with a couple hundred people chatting away. The buzz of chatter echoed in my ears and I thought I was going to pass-out. I was so nervous but, when it was my turn to speak, I walked to the podium and said, "My name is Chad and I am an alcoholic."

I talked for 30 minutes sharing my story. People laughed in spots where they identified with what I was saying, and you could hear a pin drop at other times like when I shared about how God had answered my prayers. When I finally finished there was loud applause. I saw Kevin was smiling from ear to ear. He patted me on the back when I sat down and said, "See, now that wasn't so bad was it?"

Indeed, it felt good! That began a voyage of sobriety that has lasted 38 years so far. Even though difficult things continued to happen in my life, I did not drink.

Dick died shortly after I was released on probation. I got a call one day at work from his wife that he had been rushed to the hospital. I left the office early and drove to Worcester where I found him in the intensive care unit. They would not let me see him because I was not an immediate relative. Until his wife saw me in the hall talking to the nurses and she called down the hall, "He's okay. He's my son. You can let him in."

I walked into Dick's room and he was lying in bed with I.V. lines coming out of him. And he said, "Chad, how are you? Getting to many meetings lately?"

I answered, "Dick, what is this all about? What are you doing here?"

His wife started to tell me what was wrong with him: heart failing, and arteries clogged. When Dick interrupted, "So Chad, how's the job, the wife and the kids?"

He had a big smile on his face, but I was still worried about him and I said, "Dick, the family and job are fine. When are you getting out? Let's go to a meeting."

He said, "I don't know when I'm getting out. My heart is only 20% of what it should be. But, that's okay. I should have been dead years ago. God kept me alive just long enough to see you get sober. There is a meeting at the hospital tonight. You want to go?"

I answered, "Sure, what time?"

We agreed to meet at 6:00 pm and go down to the lower floor of the hospital. I headed out to get a hamburger with the idea to return at 5:30. When I returned, Dick's wife was

4 – REVELATION

downstairs in the hospital lobby. I saw that she was weeping. She came up to me and said, "He's gone."

I comforted Dick's wife for a while. She told me that I meant a lot to him. That I was his best success story, an answer to his prayers. I just listened unsure what to think – unsure what to feel.

When I got into my car to leave, I started crying – crying hard. I found myself at a local strip joint sitting right at the dance floor. I ordered a coke and watched the woman take her clothes off. All I wanted to do was get drunk but at the same time I did not want to drink. Instead, I heard Dick saying that God kept him alive long enough to see me get sober. The woman was naked except for a G-string. She was bent over and reaching out to me with both hands. I got up, the bouncer came over to me and she backed off. I just left, got into my car and drove home still sober.

During this time, our daughter Kate was having difficulty sleeping. I would lay with her at night until she fell asleep. One night, while I was lying there next to her on her bed she said," Daddy, why is it that every time I stay at Auntie's house Joey puts his penis in my mouth?"

Sean was five years old and Kate was three when I went to prison. For a year he and his sister were left at my aunt's house when Sharon needed a babysitter. Grievously, my Aunt's teenage son Joey sexually molested both Sean and Kate. We did not find out about what had happened to our children until that evening when Kate told me what Joey was doing to her.

It is an understatement to say that I was horrified by Kate's news. After a moment's hesitation I was able to respond to her, "I don't know why he does that, honey. But I promise you that will never happen again. Do you believe me?" She looked at me with total trust and nodded. A moment later she fell asleep. No doubt relieved after having finally spoken up.

I, however, did not feel very good. I got up from my daughter's bed and went downstairs where I wept. I was shaking uncontrollably and physically sick in the living room. To this day I cannot begin to describe all the feelings that flooded over me. But I wanted to strike out at Joey, my Aunt, my Uncle, and I wanted to just scream. It occurred to me through all of this that my precious daughter was carrying all this emotion around the whole time I was away and months after I got home. No wonder she was having trouble sleeping. In fact, Sharon and I began to have a better understanding of the other behavioral issues Kate was experiencing.

When my wife and I went to bed that evening, I still could not tell her what Kate shared with me. It was not until the next day, when I confronted my Aunt and my nephew Joey, that I was able tell my wife. As if my daughter's ordeal was not enough, Joey told me that he had also molested our son Sean!

When I asked Sean about it, he shrugged his shoulders and denied any knowledge that anything happened to him. We hired

4 – REVELATION

child psychiatrists to talk to our children and I went to the police about Joey. Joey went to jail and was put on the sex offenders register. Sharon and I went on to try to repair the damage.

Even after all these years it is difficult for me to write about this period of our lives. I find myself wanting to cover it quickly and move on. The psychiatrists said that Sean seemed to have no memory of any sexual abuse. However, as Sean got older his behavior became more troublesome.

At thirteen years old he was sneaking out of the house at night to do God knows what. One Thanksgiving he told me someone dropped a tab of acid (LSD) in his drink at a party he attended the day before. After that, he began using mind altering substances regularly, smoked marijuana, and he began to have trouble in school, totaled a couple of my cars and was disruptive at home. One morning Sharon and I started to take the stairs down to the kitchen and there, lying at the foot of the stairs on the floor, was Sean. Sharon screamed and I began to call 911 when Sean rolled over and groaned. Later when he sobered up, I confronted him. He denied even being there on the floor. He even accused me of overreacting. This sort of thing kept happening. Although Sean accused me of overreacting it got so bad that my wife and I started talking about taking him out of school to get him away from the drugs.

I'm was not sure what was going on back then. Because, every now and then Sean would surprise me. For instance, when

Amend a Broken Mind

he was 13 years old, he gave me a card on my birthday that contained the following handwritten note:

Daddy you're the greatest,

Whenever I need you, you're there.

Sometimes I need help with my homework,

You always come through in the end.

One time I hit my head,

Blood was coming out.

You said I'd be alright,

You knew just what to do.

I know it's very true that you,

Always come through in the end.

Remember riding my bike?

You said I could ride like the wind.

That may be an exaggeration,

But true is my love for you.

I'm glad to have you as a daddy,

I really and truly am.

When God handed out the fathers,

I got the best!

4 – REVELATION

On the heels of this note from Sean and not knowing what else to do, I went to the principal of the high school to tell him about the problems we were having with Sean and about the drugs available in his school. His response was, "What do you expect me to do about it? That's your problem."

I had visions of the old days when someone in power rudely pushed my concerns aside. However, instead of becoming full of resentment and anger Sharon and I decided to pursue other options. I took Sean to a few local private schools and talked to the headmasters. They seemed interested in Sean. However, Sean was not at all interested in any of them. So, we asked God for help and we took Sean out of high school to home school him hoping to get him away from the drugs.

Unfortunately, this was back in the early nineteen nineties and the home-schooling movement was in its infancy. The principal, with whom I visited previously to talk about Sean's access to drugs, contacted us and threatened to turn us over to the police if Sean was not sent back to the school. He threatened to have our children taken away from us. He said he was very concerned about what taking our son out of school would do to Sean.

The police did come by and we were forced to get an attorney to defend ourselves. We discovered HSLDA. Home School Legal Defense Association was formed in the early 1980s when two attorneys and homeschooling dads—Mike

Amend a Broken Mind

Farris and Mike Smith—saw the need to provide low cost method of obtaining quality legal defense. In their own words:

> *Through many families sticking together, we have been able to keep the cost of a year's membership close to the rate that a family would have to pay for an hour of an attorney's time almost anywhere else...The age-old concept of parents teaching their children at home had fallen into obscurity. Families who chose such a "nontraditional" education route often encountered opposition, sometimes even legal challenges, from the educational bureaucracy as well as from their own friends and relatives.* [2]

Soon, the school and police left us alone and we taught Sean the normal high school subjects and tried to manage his behavior issues. At one point, using the carrot and stick method of discipline, we reached the almost laughable point where Sean was prohibited from using the phone, prohibited from going out of the house alone, and grounded indefinitely. We sent him to one psychiatrist or councilor after another, pushed him to get a driver's license, and forced him to get a part time job. We did everything we could think of. He fought us every step of the way.

Once the attorneys at HSLDA managed to get the authorities off our back, our daughter Kate asked to be home schooled as well. We faced many lectures from friends, neighbors and even people we did not know who felt it was their duty to approach

4 – REVELATION

us and tell us how they believe our children would be irreparably damaged by being isolated from public school. Often, we would be asked what we were doing about socialization and what were we going to do about high school diplomas and college entrance requirements? Our efforts were not totally wasted, though. Sean finished the curriculum that we had and later, after he moved out of the house, he sent me a Father's Day card that said, "I love you Dad. Remember the time you grounded me forever?"

When Sean was finished with our curriculum, we had him take a GED high school equivalency test. He passed and was given a high school diploma. Then we had him take the SAT college exams. To our great surprise and relief, he scored in the top 10 percentile without any preparation. We went to the principal who had earlier expressed his real concern for our son's future and asked him if he would write a recommendation to be included in Sean's college applications. He refused.

We were forced to send out college applications without letters of recommendations from school officials or official transcripts. The applications contained only an essay written by Sean and his SAT results. The result was, he was accepted at every college to which we sent applications. Northeastern University gave Sean a generous scholarship and he accepted their offer for the coming Fall term.

His mother and I got him installed in the dorms that Fall of 1994. He had a job in the school to help him with spending

Amend a Broken Mind

money. His classroom focus was going to be on English studies. After a few weeks I went to see how he was doing. He was in his dorm with a couple other young men playing their guitars. Sean said, "Hey Dad, listen to this."

He began singing, to the rock and roll beat provided by the accompaniment of his friends, "Sittin' in my cat box contemplatin' my navel." Then, after a few verses of that they switched to a disco rhythm and Sean repeated the refrain, "Sittin' in my cat box, and contemplatin' my navel," with a Disco beat. This was followed, a few verses later, by the same song only this time sung to a Country rhythm with steel guitar strains, "Sittin' in my cat box after loosin' my pick-up truck and my girl and contemplating my navel." Finally, they finished with a Reggae rhythm of the same verses, "Sittin' in my cat box Man, smokin' a bong and contemplatin' my navel." At the time, I laughed along with them at the cleverness of it all.

The phrase "Sittin' in my cat box contemplatin' my navel" came from a dinner conversation we had at home a year of two earlier, before Sean started at Northeastern. It was inspired by a story on the radio about a man in India who had been sitting in a box in the living room of his home for five years not speaking, washing, or taking care of any of his bodily needs. I was telling my wife and children at the dinner table about the man and how his wife fed him, bathed him and cleaned up after him. She also worked and took care of their six children. I was, at the time, mocking the man's religion and his decision to abandon his family in the pursuit of that religion. I came up with the phrase

4 – REVELATION

and melody "Sittin' in my cat box contemplatin' my navel" at the dinner table.

Two terms into his freshman year Sean got a letter from the Dean telling him he was on academic suspension. Apparently, he rarely attended classes and his teachers gave him incomplete or failing grades. I had no idea that he was skipping classes and when I asked him what the problem was, he responded, "The teachers here are idiots."

AMEND A BROKEN MIND

5 – SEAN'S COLLEGE CAREER

Hi, my name is Sean D'Amour. My Dad asked me to write down my recollections of my childhood up to now. Like, I tried to write but I can't. My hand is too shaky because of the damn meds I have to take.

He and Mom are upset because I won't sign the documents that the hospital put in front of me. The papers supposedly will allow the hospital to tell my parents what my treatment is and like what the hospital says is wrong with me. I decided that this hospital bull shit had to stop after the last hospitalization when my Dad drove me around from one hospital to another while the Dominican gang was following us. I'm not sick and don't need medication, shrinks, counselors, or any of that stuff. Besides, the Dominicans are like probably still trying to find out where I am.

But I'm getting ahead of myself. I was born in 1976 in Marblehead, Massachusetts after my father finished a bachelor's degree from a local college. The earliest memory I have is being pulled along the streets of Marblehead in a sled after a May blizzard. There were no cars on the road because the snow was like five feet deep and everyone in town was out walking the streets. I remember that despite the snow that was keeping everyone from doing what they wanted, it was a happy time with everyone unable to go to work and walking around town with a smile on their face. My Dad had 10 days off from work because he was unable to get to the office. Me and my

Mom and Dad walked to the beach to watch the waves crash onto the shore. We walked downtown to shop for food in the half empty stores. We visited like every seaside park in town and played in the snow.

Who knows, some of my memory comes from listening to stories told by my parents and other people. But it was a good time, at least in my memory. Before the real shit storm hit.

I remember when my Dad came home from jail. I was told at the time that he was in the hospital. But later he told me what happened and where he really was. I think I was 13 when he told me the truth. It didn't affect me while he was away because I was like real young but later, as I got old enough to go out into the neighborhood I was teased and bullied a lot by kids about my Dad being an ex-con and rapist (at least that what the kids called him). I eventually just stayed away from the kids in the neighborhood. I often wished that we could like move. But I never said anything.

After my Dad was home for a few years I remember being sent to some counselors and psychiatrists. Although I did not know what they were at the time, I came to understand later that my Mom and Dad were worried about how Dad's incarceration and the molestation by Cousin Joey was affecting me. I didn't trust any of the people they sent me to. In fact, they were all idiots. Also, I don't remember Joey doing anything to me so I would just sit there and say nothing.

AMEND A BROKEN MIND

When I got into my teen years, I remember going on a Christian camping trip in Pennsylvania called Creation. I went with the youth group from our church. We camped out for like a week and listened to speakers and bands. I spent most of the time wandering around at night meeting girls and smoking dope. When we came home, I could not sit still. I wanted the freedom I had at Creation and wanted to smoke more weed. My parents were not too pleased with this. I got really angry. Sometimes I just like snapped, and a wave of fury poured out of me. I would scream and punch holes in walls in the house. My Dad patiently made me patch the holes. He did most of the work though. I just stood there and thought about getting away somehow.

It was around this time that I found a group of guys who liked to smoked dope and hung around homes with no parents present (divorced or both working) listening to music and messing around with girls. My best friend Eddie's father and mother smoked marijuana and let Eddie smoke it when he was like 16 so I had a regular supply and loved it. Why couldn't I have parents like Eddie's. Okay, I didn't know it then, but I admit it now, (or at least admit that everyone tells me) I was self-medicating.

Marijuana and pills helped quiet the anxiety that I felt almost all the time I was not smoking or on some pill. It seemed to quiet the anger too. I think it was also around this time that I started like seeing angels and hearing voices. I had a bedroom at home on the third floor (it's my Dad's law office now). It was

5 – Sean's College Career

easy to climb out a window and let myself down from the roof. So, I snuck out a lot especially when I was grounded (which was often).

I remember when my Dad got this outside sales job. He started traveling a lot for work and was like not around as much to control me. My Mom spent most days home schooling Kate and my youngest sister Flo when he traveled. I really took advantage of the freedom and snuck out often. Mom didn't notice. She stayed home and did her thing. I slept all day and went out like all night. It worked for me.

Occasionally, I saw angels when I was high. Sometimes I saw them when I wasn't high too – usually when I was in bed. I also heard voices that told me that my parents were dick heads and it was okay to lie to them, okay to take my Mom's medications, and okay to take any money I could find in their bedroom. The angels, though, were cool. I told my sister about them once and she said I should tell Dad. I made her promise not to say anything. If he knew, he would really think I was like crazy or accuse me of being on drugs.

I remember having trouble with my sexual identity too. It wasn't as popular a subject as it is now, and no one talked about it. But my Dad must have noticed something because he talked to me about it a couple of times. I would take my Mom's underclothes and like wear them in my room. Or, go out wearing a dress. I still didn't remember Joey doing anything to me.

Amend a Broken Mind

The voices were sometimes a problem. Like when my parents were talking to me, it would sometimes feel like there was a whole room of people like speaking at the same time. I'd get like really confused and my Dad would get even more frustrated with me. Sure, I never said anything to him about the voices and angels. But I did try to tell him about how the Fed. (sic. Federal Reserve Bank) is a front for a group of foreigners whose purpose is to fund wars and enforce the iron will of the new world order through banking control. I told him where he could get the facts and he like blew me off. He never believes anything I say!

Looking back, things may have been better at home if I shared with them what was going on in my life. But, I listened to bands like Green Day who sang about not being part of the Prozac Nation (like my Mom) and I did not want to go through like electroshock therapy like the mother in "Next to Normal" and my grandfather did. Besides, my mania was not all that unattractive. Girls seemed to think I was sexy and cool. I wasn't about to give up being cool and different just so my parents could have a happy home.

I never told my parents about the anxiety that I lived with and was trying to avoid. I mean, the manic people in movies like "The Apartment" and "Almost Famous" were portrayed as mysterious and the treatment for mental illness was like scary (not that I am or was crazy). Besides, they wouldn't understand, and I would end up in some idiot shrink's office.

5 – Sean's College Career

I once brought this rap CD home from the library that had the words, "Your mom's a bitch so just kill her. Take a butcher knife from the kitchen and hack her to bits." (Laughs)

I don't know, I thought it was funny. My ex-con Dad made a big stink about it though. He went to the library and gave them hell for letting kids take out that sort of stuff. It was hard for me to take him seriously considering what he did, going to prison and all.

One year at Christmas time my dad did this mock Christmas card. It was like a take-off on the letters that sometimes came to the house with cards from friends or relatives. They share all the wonderful things that happen during the past year. Like, they would say, "Johnny graduated from Harvard this year and spent the summer traveling in Europe while Betty like sang the blues at Carnegie Hall. All the critics loved her!"

My Dad's card, however, went something like this, "Merry Christmas from the D'Amours. We have had a typical year. Sean continues to reject everything his parents stand for while sneaking out of the house every night and frantically running up and down the stairs talking to girls on the phone, Kate (my younger sister) still wears ear plugs so she cannot hear her mother clear her throat and continues to communicate only with hand motions, Sharon (my mother) still sleeps 20 hours a day in spite of the five depression meds she takes, and Chad (my Dad) paints the house and cuts the grass so that we can look normal to the neighbors."

AMEND A BROKEN MIND

When Dad shared this with us, he couldn't stop laughing. He thought it was so clever. The rest of us just stood there and looked at him. What was he laughing at? It was like so true.

In my junior year in high school, my parents took me out of the public school to get me away from the drugs -- at least that was what they said. I know now that they took me out so that they could control me more and make themselves feel like they were being good parents. Dad taught me math and sciences and my Mom taught history and English.

As part of my home schooling they also made me get a driver's license and a job. I got a job at a Dunkin Donuts like 20 minutes away from home. I didn't want anyone I knew to see me working as part of the corporate machine. All the evil in the world is caused by those companies. They support the Prozac culture, despoil the natural world, and enslave the population. They even made the original long banana extinct by destroying all the plants and replacing them with a genetically modified smaller version that's easier to ship and could be sold for more money. And, don't get me started on the National Bank and how that is another rip-off of the people.

When I finished my high school work as a home-schooled kid in 1993 me and my Dad sent out some college applications. I did not really want to go to college, but my Dad was like pushing me to go. He said I had a powerful mind and I needed to get some education and discover what I was good at. To be

5 – SEAN'S COLLEGE CAREER

honest, I went along with him so that I could like get away from my parents, listen to music, get high, and hang out with girls.

I took the college entrance exams and my Dad was really impressed because I did good and didn't even study. On the strength of my exams and an essay that I wrote, I got accepted to Gordon College, Northeastern University and Suffolk University. All of them were local colleges. Northeastern gave me like the best deal. I had played hockey from an early age and the last year I played I was like top scorer in my league. So Northeastern gave me a hockey scholarship, a part time job and academic scholarships (at least that was what I was told). I played hockey for one season but did not like it. It was no fun with all the yelling and threats from the coaches. I didn't tell anyone, I just stopped showing up at practices after the coach was pissed at me for scoring against his favorite goalie. He was an idiot.

I never did go to the job they had for me. I can't even tell you what it was. I didn't go to classes very often either. (Laughs) Like I told my Dad, the teachers were all idiots. I hung out at the dorm and began dealing drugs. I needed some money, didn't I? The drugs led me to Canada once with like $100,000 in my pocket to pick up some pills and dope. But it was a setup. I was supposed to make the pickup at the border. The guy was there but he had a pick-up loaded with Dominicans. They took all the money, beat me up good, and left me there in the woods. I came too all sore and bruised the next morning, climbed into

Amend a Broken Mind

my car and headed back to Boston empty handed. (Pause) That really sucked.

Unfortunately, Jose, the guy that gave me the money, was expecting me to come back with the goods (Laughs). I didn't have anything but a sore ribcage and a battered face. When I got back to town, I went to see my girlfriend and told her I was jumped by Dominicans, beat up and robbed. I needed to leave town before Jose came looking for me. My girlfriend Melanie agreed that we should leave town, so she like arranged for us to ride to California with a couple of friends.

When we left Boston in our friend's Subaru it was, I think, the Summer of 1995. I was, I don't know, 19 – 20 at the time and so glad to be moving on. My college experience was not great. I met Melanie at a party in one of the dorms. She was 18 and hot. Every moment we were alone we were having sex. She also had another thing going for her. She inherited a bunch of money from her grandfather and was living on her inheritance. I told my Dad that I wanted to go to California to pursue being a professional DJ. He had already spoken to me about my grades and the fact that I was on like academic probation. I think he was just tired of trying to control me because all he said was, "I can't support you in this. You should stay here and complete college before you go off to California."

In my Dad's defense, he had no idea that the real reason I was going to California was because my life was not worth

5 – SEAN'S COLLEGE CAREER

much around Boston if Jose caught up to me and I did not have his drugs.

Melanie's friend Heike owned the car we would be riding in. He was from Finland. He was 25 years old, about six-feet tall with light blond hair and a turned-up nose. He loved to laugh and was real fun to be around. He really wanted to begin a new life in California. He got me turned onto his favorite pill, speed. He had this girlfriend named Joanne. She was about 5' 6" tall and thin with like dark hair and dark eyes. I did not know her then and still don't know anything about her because she never spoke. She loved to get high though, so she fit right in.

All this helped to distract me some from anxiety and the fear that Jose and his Dominican gang would catch up to me if I did not leave. I still find myself looking over my shoulder and hiding when I see a suspicious looking person.

AMEND A BROKEN MIND

6 – LIFE WITH SOBRIETY

Before Sean went to college, I lost the job I got when I was incarcerated. I worked there for a total of seven years. The packing industry had crashed, business dropped off quickly, and I got laid-off along with 100 other people. During those years working at inside sales, I could not help but notice the outside salespeople when they assembled at the factory for quarterly meetings. They always arrived in nice cars and seemed to laugh a lot. Whereas, I was struggling to support my family on my inside sales income. I drove an old Chevy Malibu with rusted doors that flapped in the wind when I was on the highway.

Somehow word got out about our poverty and the day before Christmas, when I came home from a part time job I had taken to supplement unemployment benefits, someone had left a Christmas tree, three bags of age appropriate gifts, and a couple of boxes of groceries including a huge turkey at our back door. Sharon and I had a tearful moment as we went through the boxes and bags that were left on our doorstep. To this day I do not know where it all came from.

Now that I was out of work, I made a new goal. I decided that I was going to become a salesman for a manufacturing company. I was offered a very good paying project management job at General Electric Corporation. but I turned it down because I was committed to this goal of being an outside salesman. Everything I read said sales was the best paying profession. I remember thinking, "I live in the richest country in the world and I am barely getting by. A sales job will change my life and the lives of my family."

So motivated and with a change of resume that focused on my technical sales abilities I confidently began the interview process. Unfortunately, it was *deja vu* all over again as I went to interviews and was not able to close the deal and get the job. I had no trouble getting interviews and this time I did not have to tell prospective employers that I was living in a prison. However, when the question came up on the application asking, "Have you ever been convicted of a felony?" I had to answer yes. That put my chances at the bottom of the pile or in the trash bucket right off. Therefore, after a half dozen interviews that fell flat, I remembered Dick MacCallum.

I was out of work for four months by the time I thought about what Dick would say if he was alive. Unemployment and the part time job were not anywhere enough for my family's needs and all my retirement savings were gone. I remember smiling when I thought about what he would say if I could go to him and ask for his advice. "Have you asked God for help?" he would say with a grin.

For some reason I did not previously think of turning to God for help with this new goal. However, that night as I went to bed I did as I know Dick would have suggested and I prayed, "God, please help me find a sales job that will support my family."

Amend a Broken Mind

It struck me at the time that people had been passing through my life during this period, touching me as maybe I had touched them – leaving something behind – like a powerful influence altering my personality. Dick was like that for me – and Rickie too. Kevin was also influential -- playing a big role in my sobriety and emotional growth.

Each morning I had the routine of driving to business parks and walking into every building there asking about jobs and leaving my resume. The day after I prayed, I left the house dressed in my business suit at 8:00 am as I had been doing every morning since I got laid off. As I drove down the main street in Beverly, I noticed a company in a building set back from the road behind a laundromat. The name mentioned circuit sales, so I stopped in the lot and prepared to go in. This time I repeated the prayer from the night before.

I went in and spoke with the receptionist. To my left was a glass wall separating me from a large room with about eight steel desks. Each desk had a phone and computer monitor and was manned by a young man gesticulating wildly and talking loudly on the phone. The outside wall was one-way glass and the whole place was reminiscent of a goldfish bowl.

The owner came down the stairs to talk to me. He was thirty something, tall and slim with dark hair. His dark eyes had no kindness in them, and the expression on his face was hard. He introduced himself as Ben. As we talked, I explained my

6 – LIFE WITH SOBRIETY

experience and accomplishments and he asked, "How much money do you want to earn?"

I answered with my best smile, "Well, I've been out of work for four months, so I will take just about anything for a chance at a sales job."

He turned, walked back up the stairs, and said over his shoulder, "You're not right for this job."

There was nothing for me to do but leave the building and go to the car. I sat there behind the wheel with the car running. A feeling of total hopelessness washed over me. In the old days I would have gotten drunk. However, I was so afraid of ending up in jail again that drinking was no longer an option. Instead, I took out my AA schedule. There was a meeting in Peabody at noon and I had time to make it.

It was a little after noon time when I arrived. I took a seat in the back and tried to compose myself as I listened to the first speaker share his experience, strength, and hope. The guy sitting next to me kept saying hi and generally acting a little odd. I ignored him the best I could until the break when he leaned over to me and asked, "How did the interview go?"

It took a minute for me to figure out what he was getting at, so he explained, "I was in the sales room at Northeast Circuit Sales when you came in. Did you get the job?"

I was still quite depressed, so I just shook my head, "No."

Amend a Broken Mind

He gestured and said, "Come outside with me."

We stepped outside the dark basement of the church into the parking lot. It was a beautiful sunny August afternoon. The guy I stepped outside with introduced himself as Todd and asked me, "What happened during the interview?"

I was grateful to have someone to talk to, so all my frustration came flooding out. I told Todd my whole story – how I had gone to prison, been released, got laid off, and have been frustrated in my effort to find a sales job. I told him, "Ben said I was not right for the job."

Todd listened quietly to me and when I had run out of words, he said, "This is what I want you to do. Tomorrow morning get on the phone and call Ben. Tell him to give you a shot. Tell him he has nothing to lose. You will work for commission only. All you need is a desk and a phone. He will give you the job. I promise. Then, this weekend, I want you to go to the library and look at the Thomas Register. Look up companies that manufacture electronic things – toys, computers, phones, radios, satnav systems, TVs, DVD players, VCR players, and anything else you can find. Write down on a 3x5 index card the company name, address, as well as name and phone number of purchasing people."

He finished with a smile. "I have to go back to work now. I'll see you Monday."

6 – LIFE WITH SOBRIETY

The next morning, Friday, I called Ben like Todd said I should, "Ben, I want you to give me a chance. You've got nothing to lose. Just give me a desk and a phone and let me show you what I can do."

He replied, "Alright hotshot. I'll see you on Monday."

That weekend, like Todd told me to do, I went to the library and collected names and addresses of companies and people involved in electronic manufacturing. I showed up at the office Monday morning with 150 index cards filled with names and phone numbers of people to contact. Ben was surprised to see me but was good to his word and gave me a desk and phone. He told me, "Call the purchasing people on your cards and ask if they need any chips."

The first call that I made was a hoot. A man answered the phone by giving his name John. I responded, "Hi John, um, ah, er, um."

My heart was pounding, and I could not get any words out. My tongue felt like lead. He asked, "Who is this?"

I responded, "This is Chad."

He replied," Well Chad, what do you want?"

"Do you need any chips?" I spit out.

Truth is, I got an order for $6,000.00 in eProm chips that first day and earned $600.00 in commission. At the end of the month I had more sales than anyone in the group and won the

Amend a Broken Mind

Salesman of the Month award. At the end of the year I had earned a little over $100,000.00 in commissions. That was in 1989.

It was a crazy, wild place to work. There was beer in the coke machine. The company hired strippers to come in and motivate us. My boss, who sat behind me, snorted coke in the office during the day. Tensions were high. I rode to work each morning with the car radio blasting as I pounded the dashboard to get my adrenalin going. As I described earlier, our office was like a fishbowl. Eight guys at desks talking fast, yelling, and slamming the phone down in anger – always trying to get 50 phone calls in every day.

One day, about a year into my time there, Ben came up with a policy that we were to tell everyone to whom we sold something that we would take back whatever they wanted to return no questions asked. "Tell them we are like Sears," Ben said.

It so happens that I had a customer the day before Ben's declaration that we were "like Sears" to whom I sent a package of resisters. The customer called after receiving the shipment to tell me that the resistors had rusted leads and he could not use them. I told him to send them back which he did. The next day, when the parts arrived Ben came into the fishbowl, stood infront of us salesmen, and yelled, "We got a package of resisters back that were sent out a couple days ago. Who the hell said the customer could return the parts?"

6 – Life with Sobriety

I stood up and said," I did."

"What fucking right do you have to authorize a return?"

I could feel the old anger stirring at being treated unjustly and responded with force, "You said we should tell our customers we were like Sears."

Ben came to my desk, swept everything off the top with his arm, looked at me and roared, "That's my fucking money you are giving away."

The vein in his neck was bulging, his face was red, and his fists were clenched. As he was cursing and jumping up and down on the stuff that he had swept to the floor. The memory of my first cell mate threatening to kill me flashed to my mind. I was feeding off Ben's anger and I was afraid I was going to hit him. Instead of striking out, I turned and left the office. I headed straight for the gym and worked my anger off by lifting weights.

That weekend I decided, "Now is a good time to look for another job."

This time a sales job came easily. I had three Best Salesmen of the Month awards and a year of sales experience in a commission only job to show a prospective employer. The very next week I interview for three jobs and was offered an outside sales position with a company that manufactured sensing devices for meteorological equipment and industrial

Amend a Broken Mind

applications. I left the magic question on the applications, "Have you been convicted of a felony?" — blank.

I quit the circuit sales job and took the offered position at the meteorological equipment manufacturer. I quickly began to make good money and reaped the benefits of company health insurance and retirement savings plans. We even bought a new car. Sharon and I were able to take the kids on family vacation for the very first time. On one trip we went to Philadelphia and toured all the historic places in the area. The thing I remember most about that trip was going out to eat in a swanky restaurant with Sean, Kate and our youngest who was two years old at the time (our AA baby we called her). Sean ordered a huge sirloin steak and enjoyed it immensely. The kids were well behaved, and we all had fun. As we walked out of the restaurant an elderly couple at the table next to us got my attention. The woman smiled at me and said, "You have a lovely family." Her husband nodded in agreement.

On another vacation trip to Arizona we visited Sharon's parents in Tucson. After staying with her parents for a week, Sharon and I rented a car and drove with the children to the Grand Canyon stopping here and there as we headed North to view the changing desert and swim in delightful pools at some of the hotels along the way. One memorable moment occurred at the Northeastern end of the Grand Canyon. We were visiting an ancient Native American settlement located right on the rim of the canyon. As we speculated on what life was like when the site was inhabited Sean noticed a very dark cloud coming

6 – LIFE WITH SOBRIETY

toward us from the Southwest right up the canyon. The storm overtook us as we watched, and it started snowing heavily. This was August and we were dressed in shorts and sneakers but that didn't matter. We all laughed happily and danced around in the snow squall. That night we ate fast food for dinner and went big-ball bowling in Williams, Arizona. Those are good memories.

It was while I was working at this outside sales job that Sean went to Northeastern University, dropped out and left for California. When Sean left for California, he was 19 years old. After he left Boston, I found out that he never went to the job that the school had provided for him as part of his scholarship. He had also stopped participating in the hockey program that was part of his scholarship package.

I forgot to mention the hockey earlier. When I got home on parole, and as time went by it was obvious to me that Sean was not getting along with his peers. I did not know why at the time. However, to give him something to do that might help him work out some anger and meet some other boys I began taking him to learn-to-skate programs and, as he got to be a better skater, I signed him up for a youth hockey team.

He loved the physical aspect of the game and, because I was at all the practices and games I got involved too. I became an assistant coach, then a coach. I enjoyed it as much as Sean did. I would skate the drills and I got to be a better skater too. As time went on Sean got better and better. The last year before college,

Amend a Broken Mind

he played center and was the highest scorer in the league. He would get control at the drop of the puck and tear down the ice to score. This fact helped him get the hockey scholarship at Northeastern.

Sean was also bullied a lot in junior high school. He would come home bruised, scratched-up and angry from other boys picking on him. When I realized that this was a regular thing, I began teaching him to box. A couple times a week we would tie on the gloves and spend a half an hour punching each other. I showed him how to stand, how to hold his hands, how to defend himself and how to attack. This went on until he was 17 years old when one day as we were sparing, I took a right from him on the side of the head. It nearly knocked me out. Once the stars cleared up and I found my glasses I said, "Okay, I think you have learned all that I can teach you."

He didn't come home beat up anymore after we started the boxing lessons.

As far as I can tell, Sean started doing drugs in high school, probably when he was 16 years old — maybe earlier. I did not know until much later that his best friend Eddie smoked dope at home with his parents who were old hippies and saw nothing wrong with it. This habit continued after high school and, instead of working at the school job, he began dealing pills and dope on the campus.

After Sean left Northeastern University he went with his girlfriend and some friends to Oakland, California. He was there

6 – LIFE WITH SOBRIETY

for six years. I visited him every three months or so to see how he was doing (I was traveling to Northern California on business regularly at the time). He was sharing an apartment with a young woman named Melanie. Each time I visited him he seemed to have a different job. Occasionally, he would send home a marketing blurb advertising a show in which he was featured as a DJ. Other than my visits and his occasional marketing outreach, we did not hear from him.

When he returned from California in 2002 there was no notice, he just showed up alone on our doorstep at Thanksgiving time. He said that he had an apartment in Boston and told me that he was going to settle there. He said, "I'm done with California."

He seemed tense and anxious to please. Six months later he visited us again. This time he had a new girlfriend, Connie, in tow and told us they were getting married. We had a nice time meeting the very young and attractive girl. She was eight years younger than Sean. But they looked happy together. Sean requested that I make my home-made pancakes for dinner. I prepared a dinner of my special butter milk pancakes with bacon, home-made maple syrup, fresh berries and all.

As we ate, we learned that they met during a Rave in Boston at which Sean was the DJ. He told me a little about his DJ experience. He said, "Dad, it is the most wonderful feeling to be up on the stage with a crowd moving to the music that I create. I feed on the electricity in the crowd. The music seems to get

Amend a Broken Mind

under my skin and produce an out-of-body experience. I have been sharpening my beats and remixing over the past seven years. I have a record collection of a few thousand recordings and my own equipment. The future looks awesome."

He described working under a haunting pink hue while he tended his machinery, hands poised above the knobs. He claimed his body was carried by the sound, hips oscillating, his hair in his face, his arms outstretched, like at worship. As he was describing his experience, I was wondering what this rave business was all about.

Wanting to discover what Raves were, I did some on-line research. It seems that the idea originated in London in the 1950s. At that time the term Rave described bohemian parties that London, Soho beatniks threw. Later, the Rave medium had been used by musicians like Buddy Holly, and David Bowie. Electronic music began using the Rave venue as a name for huge underground acid house events that drew thousands of people and spawned an entire subculture. "Raving" was entirely centralized around underground dance music. Not anything you would hear on top 40 radio. [3]

As with most movements open to the public there are those who idealize the activity so that it takes on an almost religious aura. These folks tend to look down on the individuals who use the Rave as a place to get sloppy drunk, high on ecstasy and moly and pick up a sex partner. In fact, one can go on-line and find the 10-steps on how to behave at your first Rave. However,

6 – LIFE WITH SOBRIETY

the general reputation is of an all-night party in a dirty warehouse, stoned out of your mind, half naked and very cool. [4]

Sean and Connie told Sharon and me that they were going to get married. The wedding was eventually held at the bride's stepfather's golf club. The pastor officiating was Sean's pastor whose son was one of Sean's best friends growing up. Sean also made the music selection and he had a friend handle the DJ work. Once the ceremony, meal and toasts were out of the way the wedding took on the spirit of a Rave. There was an open bar, and everyone danced wildly to Sean's music selection. Most everyone got good and drunk. Sean and his new bride were all smiles. They made a very handsome couple. Photos of the event still bring a smile to my face. After the reception they flew to Sanibel Island, Florida (a wedding gift from Sharon and me) for a one-week honeymoon. Seven months later Sean's new wife gave birth to a little girl.

Much later we found out that Sean and his new wife agreed with each other that they would stop selling and doing drugs when the baby was born. However, neither one of them had any skills to support themselves and the drugs had a greater hold on each of them than they realized.

Furthermore, the Rave scene was one that depended on drugs to produce the euphoria of the event. Consequently, Sean started dealing drugs again (or never stopped) to support the family and to support their individual habits. Two years later, in

AMEND A BROKEN MIND

2005, they divorced, shared child custody, and Sean tried to pay a level of child support that he could not afford.

Before the divorce, I tried to talk to each of them and get them to work out their differences. However, she had put up with enough. She said that she was afraid of his anger and he accused her of on-line sexting. He also accused her of running an on-line sex ring. I really did not understand any of this at the time. But in retrospect I think his delusions and paranoia were part of the dissolution of the marriage. I ended up paying for his lawyer.

In retrospect it seems to me that this divorce was a watershed incident in Sean's life. He obviously was devastated by the divorce and estrangement from his adored daughter. He began to lose jobs shortly after he started them. The year after his divorce Sean had 13 different jobs – a clear indication (at least I thought it was) of a slide into depression.

Amend a Broken Mind

7 – Angels Everywhere

Hey there, it's Sean again. It was the 4th of July maybe eight years after my divorce. I was in my late-thirties and my girlfriend Maureen and I were on our way to the fireworks with my two kids (one with Connie and one with Maureen), and my parents in my parent's SUV when the most incredible thing happened. It was like a beautiful clear evening. The windows in the SUV were open to the muggy air. The smell of freshly mowed hay was in the air. The crickets were chirping loud enough to hear over the road noise. It wasn't dark outside yet and the colors were so vibrant – like they were singing. Everything was looking vibrant -- more real than real.

It felt like we were driving through one of those surrealistic paintings from the 1800s. You know, the ones with women posing in flowing robes on cliffs with roman columns everywhere surrounded by a glowing sky. I was sitting in the back seat and, I'll tell you, when I first looked up, I couldn't believe what I was seeing--but it was so real. It was as real as you are to me. When I looked up to the sky, I saw angels. They were flying in random directions overhead. I excitedly yelled and pointed to the sky, "Look at the angels!"

The joking around that usually went along with these outings with my parents suddenly stopped. My father said, "Oh Sean, you mean the jets flying overhead?"

Man was he annoying! I said with more force in my voice, "No, I see angels. They are definitely angels!"

There was a slight pause, and everyone began talking over me like nothing unusual was going on. But I was drawn more and more to the incredible sight outside.

I'd seen angels off and on over the years, but this was different. When we got to the fireworks area, we climbed up the gently sloping hay field to the top. It was a very nice New England scene. The fireworks would be set off in the small valley below where the narrow road winded through the valley floor. Crowds of people congregated down there. Some were in their cars working their way along the road to the parking fields. Others were wandering around the food and trinket stalls. Still others were waiting in line to use the porta-potties. Music throbbed from a loud rock band on a temporary stage covered by an awning.

We spread our blankets on the hillside in the freshly cut hay and opened the picnic basket to begin our supper. We were surrounded by the sounds and smells from band, insects, hay and food from below. Overhead, stars started appearing in the sky as dusk moved in. Along with the stars, splashes of colored light winked on and off in the sky when two of the angels crossed paths and it seemed all so comfortable and reasonable. I wondered why everyone wasn't looking up. It was an awesome spectacle that filled me with a wicked feeling of joy.

Quietly I said, "They are angels."

My 10-year old daughter snapped at me, "Daddy, stop it!"

AMEND A BROKEN MIND

My Dad thinks I'm crazy. But, like I tell him repeatedly, the things I see are as real as he is. He just doesn't believe me. He never believes anything I say. Like the time the Costa Rican drug lord and his gang were in the woods behind the house. They were there I tell you! When I finally convinced him to look, my father claimed he couldn't see them. I told him that's because of the invisibility cloaks they wear. He just kept insisting there is no such thing as an invisibility cloak and insisted that I go to the hospital again.

Like, that's his answer for everything – go to the hospital! We've been to the hospital a million times before. All they do is put me on drugs and make me sit through boring group sessions. They don't believe me either. When I talk to them it's like they seem to hear something else and when they talk back there are so many voices in my head, like I can't understand half of what they are saying.

I should never have shown my Dad the video I took of my keyboard levitating while I was at work. Of course, he denied seeing the keyboard rise. It was so obvious! Even my boss saw it!

My relationship with my Dad has been uncomfortable for me since he got home from prison. I was, I think, five when my father came home. I remember my Mom was all excited and we tied yellow ribbons around the tree in the front yard to welcome him home. At the time I did not know what it meant but when I came down in the morning, he was in the kitchen having coffee.

7 – ANGELS EVERYWHERE

He looked up and smiled and I said, "What are you doing here?"

He did try to reconnect with me but the years after his return were very difficult. All the neighborhood kids teased me mercilessly about my father being a convict. I never said anything to him about it, but his being sent to jail and the publicity surrounding it affected our relationship. Ever since I can remember I have struggled with weird ideas regarding eating, anxiety, feeling real sad, concerns about my sexual orientation, and being unable to relax. Oh yeah, and I have trouble sleeping.

Anyway, after I showed him the video on the keyboard levitating, I agreed to go with him and my Mom to the hospital again. I knew I wasn't crazy, but I agreed just to keep the peace. I had to sit on the floor in the back seat of the car because I knew that the Dominican gang was following us. At the first hospital I saw Juan was inside in the lobby. I told my parents that I could not go in because Juan was there, and they reluctantly left. It was dark and evil in there! I could sense the evil.

We went to another hospital further away. I stayed low in the back seat of the car and peaked back every now and then. It was no use. The gang had a bead on us and were following us at every turn. I had my dad take sudden changes in directions to throw them off. We even lost them at one point after making a U-turn on the main street (Laughs). It felt good for a minute but when we pulled up to the next hospital, they were inside waiting for me.

They want to get rid of me because I know all about them and their plans. I hacked into their emails and have been monitoring them for years now. But even more, they are after my girlfriend. She has given them a key to my parent's house and Juan sneaks in at night like when I am away at work. Of course, she denies it. But I'm not stupid. I know the code she uses. She ties a handkerchief on the back-door knob to let him know he can come in. I even found a used condom on the floor in the bedroom when I came back from work.

Getting back to the ride to the hospital, my parents agreed, again reluctantly, to go to another hospital. A few hours later, after many detours and backtracks to avoid detection we pulled up to a hospital that we had not stopped at yet. I peeked over the door to look inside and no one was there except a nurse. I still could not bring myself to go inside. Finally, my dad went in and got two attendants to come out to the car. When they saw that I did not want to go in on my own, they backed off hands waving in the air like they were surrendering and went inside the hospital leaving me where I was.

By this time my Dad was very frustrated. He is usually very laid back, but I could sense the tension. He told me I needed to go inside. He told me that the delusions were back just like before and he would not let me back home until I got help. I looked around and said, "I don't feel safe here."

7 – ANGELS EVERYWHERE

He pointed out a security vehicle parked right in front of us and there was obviously no one in the lobby inside the hospital, and no one was like trying to force me. I reminded him that they were using invisibility cloaks to hide themselves.

I thought he was going to explode when he heard that, but he just sighed and said that there is no such thing as invisibility cloaks. I was getting agitated now. I told him he never believes me and just thinks I'm crazy. He won't even do like research or anything on the cloaks that the army has developed. At that, he took out his smart phone and said, "Okay, will you believe Google?"

He typed in the word invisibility cloak. There was no mention of the army. Although, Harry Potter invisibility cloaks did come up as a result of the search.

He told me again to go inside. I looked around and this time it did seem safe there. A security vehicle was parked right out front and it seemed like the front door was lit by the sun in a welcoming way. He said, "Do you want me to go in with you?"

I said, "No", and got out of the car, and went into the hospital. My parents waited for a half an hour outside (I could see them watching from the car).

After the intake procedure, I was given some valium and suddenly my head cleared, and the chaos subsided. By this I mean that I heard only one voice at a time. The conviction that I

Amend a Broken Mind

was being followed ceased, my anxiety left, and I no longer believed that my girlfriend was cheating on me.

Once in the assigned hospital room, I called my father's cell phone. He did not answer but I left a message telling him that I was going to do everything I could to get to the bottom of this; that I did not want to live like this anymore; that I was so sorry for what I was doing to him and Mom; but the things I was seeing were as real to me as he is. I told him that I loved him. And, that is all I remember because I slept for the first time in three days.

8 – Oxycontin

Sean continued to live in Boston after the divorce where his daughter visited his apartment on the weekends. By the year 2010 he had found another woman with whom he lived in an apartment in Lawrence, Massachusetts. He had a job doing collections at a company near where he lived and in 2011, he and his girlfriend had a little boy. Things seemed to finally be going well for Sean. He seemed happy when he visited us with the young woman and his two children. His relationship with his ex-wife was not good but he paid his child support and regularly had visitation with his daughter.

Sean and his girlfriend applied for and received MassHealth insurance and he used it to go to a dentist for the first time in many years. The dentist said Sean needed to get his wisdom teeth out and this Sean did. Unfortunately, the dentist gave him a large bottle of Oxycontin to help mitigate the pain during recovery. Sean discovered that the opium-based pain killer helped him with his anxiety as well as with the pain of the tooth removal and the stress of supporting a family, paying child support, and dealing with his dysfunctional ex-wife. The bottle of pain killers was supposed to last a month. After a week and a half, the bottle was empty, and Sean was on the street in the evenings looking for more. It was there that he learned how to melt down the pills in a spoon and inject the liquid into his shoulder.

As his dependence on Oxycontin deepened, Sean's mental health began to worsen. Or, his ability to hide his illness weakened. I will never know which it was. He had been admitted to the mental health unit of five different hospitals since his divorce. However, he always seemed to bounce back, and I was hopeful after each stay.

It is significant then that one day in 2012, after years of ups and downs, I had to once again take him to the hospital with persistent delusions and suicidal thoughts. He spent three days in the hospital under 24-hour surveillance and was transferred to a mental health facility that resembled a converted estate. There he began detoxing from the Oxycontin and receiving treatment in the form of various medications, group counseling, one-on-one counseling, as well as training in Eastern mysticism and meditation.

When he first arrived at the facility, Sharon and I went to visit him. We were led into a stark meeting room with a metal table surrounded by half a dozen metal chairs. After about 10 minutes Sean was brought in. He immediately started talking quickly in a low conspiratorial voice and waved his hands around. "I need to get out of here. It's not safe. There are demons in my room. One of them was floating over my bed and came crashing down on me!" Sean's hand chopped down onto the table with a bang. "The demon broke the bed in half -- just like that!"

Amend a Broken Mind

Sean's eyes were darting around unable to look at us.

"It's not safe here!" He repeated.

Sharon looked horrified and my heart was pounding. We weren't sure how to answer.

I asked Sean, "When did this happen?"

He replied, "Just last night."

I said, "Is the bed still broken?"

He looked at me angrily and said, "You don't believe me, do you? You never believe anything I say! You're a fucking asshole! This visit is over."

He stormed out of the room while Sharon and I sat there wide eyed looking at each other. Sharon was crying quietly. I was stunned.

Then a ward worker came in and asked with a smile, "So, how was your visit?"

I looked at her in confusion. Did she not hear Sean yelling at us? I answered her," He claims there are demons in his room and one of them broke his bed."

She smiled and said, "I can assure you; his bed is not broken."

8 – OXYCONTIN

That was all she said. We just sat there looking at each other until Sharon and I asked her to show us out. We drove home in silence.

Back at home both my wife and I were bothered by a continuous underlying anxiety. Our discussion kept going over and over, round and round, about what should we do when Sean was released. As always happens, the dreaded moment finally arrived after 30 days in the mental health facility. It began with several phone calls and emails from Sean. All of them tailored to convince us that he had completely recovered. He promised to get a job and begged us to let him return home. He promised to follow an outpatient program designed to help him continue to receive treatment and work toward independence.

One councilor told me, "Sean presents well."

This statement was indeed correct. However, we were seeing a long persistent slide into deepening mental illness. His efforts to get us to take him back worked this time but he was becoming less and less able to maintain a façade of normalcy for any length of time.

Sean was very repentant, and his pleading melted my heart. Even though friends were encouraging us to use what they called tough love and refuse to let him stay with us we finally agreed to let him come home. All was well for a few months. He did present well. He got a job, attended the outpatient sessions, the drug screenings, and kept up with his drug prescriptions. He seemed to be doing well until, after a few

AMEND A BROKEN MIND

months, I noticed a change in behavior in line with a pattern that was becoming all too familiar. He began sleeping during the days he did not have to work and staying up all night acting agitated and going in and out of the house talking to himself and yelling at the air. Then he lost his job.

It is interesting to note that the first few months at this last job selling phone services Sean won all sorts of awards and bonuses. However, he was unable to maintain the necessary level of focus and finally lost the job when he showed to his boss a video of the keyboard on his computer levitating. He and his girlfriend and children moved in with Sharon and me because the girl friend was out of work too and they could not pay for their apartment.

On his last day at the job he was driving his sister's little Fiesta home, when he lost control of the car and hit a high curb destroying the front tires, the front wheels, and the front axle. He left the car where it was in the median and started walking. As he walked it became dark and he claimed to have crossed a field where a coven of devil worshipers was having a ritual. According to Sean, they were dancing around a fire while one of them was cutting up animals to burn on the altar.

When he got home, he was convinced that the coven (as he called the group in the field) had buried their altar in front of our mailbox. Sean came into the house and ignored the place we had set for him at the dinner table. Instead, he moved quickly around the house with a very determined look on this face. We

8 – OXYCONTIN

always sat together as a family at the dinner table and my wife, my son's girlfriend, his children and I were at the table listening as Sean stormed around the house as if all life depended on what he was doing.

He left the house with a shovel and a large plastic bucket. He began to dig up the area between the street and the mailbox and put the dirt in a bucket. It was an odd feeling to sit at the dinner table with his girlfriend and children eating the dinner my wife Sharon had prepared while Sean was outside digging up part of the yard.

The dinner conversation was stilted. We were all uneasy. No one was sure what to say about what was going on outside. The children looked confused and a little frightened. His girlfriend rolled her eyes as if to say, "There he goes again."

Sharon looked at me, "Please, do something," she pleaded.

Through the dining room windows. I could see Sean carrying the bucket over to the stone wall at the back of the yard. Having disposed of the altar, he came into the house for a bucket of white paint and a brush. After a few worried looks from my wife I followed him outside to see what he was up to. He had painted odd symbols around the pile of rubble at the stone wall. He then went to the street behind the house and painted a similar symbol. It was then the police drove up.

The officers told him to stop painting on the street and watched as Sean went in the house and got black paint to cover the symbols he just made. This process seemed to defuse the situation and when Sean came in, he acted as if nothing had happened.

As usual the process of preparing for bed was a time that Sharon and I talked about things on our mind. She asked me what we should do about Sean's increasingly bizarre behavior. I promised to talk to him the next morning about getting some help for his delusions.

Later that evening, I woke up feeling apprehensive. It was 1 a.m. and my son Sean was standing next to my bed looking down at me. When he saw that I was awake he said, "Dad, come quick. There's a demon downstairs under the dining room table."

I mumbled, "Huh, what are you talking about?"

He repeated insistently with alarm in his voice. "Come quick."

The hair stood up on the back of my neck and a feeling of dread creeped over me as I got out of bed. I looked at my wife. She was awake too. Her eyes were wide with anxiety. I went down to the kitchen and Sean was crouched on the floor behind the island. He reached up to pull me down to his level. The house was dark, lit only by the full moon.

Sean peered around the island and said, "Look, they are under the table."

8 – OXYCONTIN

Again, the hair stood up on the back of my neck and I got a chill. I was looking for some rational explanation but finally realized something was terribly wrong. I replied, "Sean, there are no demons under the table."

He replied quickly, "Look, now they are outside. You can see their red eyes looking in the windows."

Stepping out from behind the island I turned on the light. Sean was very agitated. "They are out there I tell you!" he yelled. "You never believe anything I say."

He slammed the door as he stormed out of the house. Standing on the side of the road in the light of the moon, he screamed at the house and at me. "I will destroy you! You fucking asshole! I will destroy this fucking house. I will destroy you. I will destroy everyone and everything you care about!"

My heart was pounding in my chest. I felt fear. Sean was visible through the curtains. Shaking his fist at the house, he jumped up and down, and flailed his arms in the air as he continued his rant. Suddenly, he got into one of the cars and screeched out of the driveway down the street. The night became very quiet. My heart was pounding.

After Sean left, Maureen asked if she and the children could stay with us. She said she was afraid to be alone with the children in their apartment. Sharon and I agreed to let them stay

Amend a Broken Mind

the night with us. My mind was a jumble of thoughts and feelings as I went upstairs to bed and tried to sleep.

An hour later the house phone rang. My wife and I lurched for the phone at the same time. It was Sean. He was speaking conspiratorially and asking for help. "Dad, please, call the cops. I'm trapped. They've got me surrounded!"

I said, "Who has you surrounded?"

He replied, "There are helicopters overhead and armed rangers surrounding me. They are coming to get me. Please help."

"Okay, stay on the line. Where are you?" I asked.

He whispered frantically back to me, "I'm in a parking garage in Cambridge. "

I have since been told repeatedly by the police, court clinicians, and psychiatrists that there is no law against being crazy. The authorities can only force an adult to go to the hospital if he is suicidal or violent. Otherwise, they can only take him if he asks for help. Now, over the phone, he was asking for help, so I picked up my wife's phone and called the local police. They hooked me up with the Cambridge police at the same time Sean was still on the other line.

Sean did not know where he was with any certainty other than a parking garage somewhere in Cambridge. However, he was certain that the helicopters overhead and massed armed

8 – OXYCONTIN

rangers would be easy to spot. The police traced his phone. Eventually, over the open phone line, I finally heard the Officers putting him in the back seat of their cruiser. They thanked me and told me that he was safe now. Then I overheard one of the officers ask Sean, "What do you have in the bottle?"

Sean said, "My prescription. See!"

The police took Sean to Boston City Hospital for overnight and the next day Sean was moved to a mental health facility. Sharon and I were very confused about what Sean was experiencing so we did some investigating and discovered NAMI (National Alliance on Mental Illness). NAMI [5] offers support and education programs for families and individuals living with mental health conditions. Sharon and I signed up for a six-week program with other parents and loved-ones of people in the throes of mental illness. We learned a lot of what our son was going through. We also learned that other parents were encountering the same type of behavior as we were experiencing with Sean. Sometimes the struggles we shared were uncannily similar right down to the words our mentally ill loved ones used with us.

One question that I struggled with was, "What caused all of this paranoia, anxiety, and delusion in Sean?"

Some sources claimed drug use did not cause mental illness. These sources claimed that illegal drug use was an effort by the mentally ill person to self-treat their symptoms. Other sources

AMEND A BROKEN MIND

claimed illegal drug use changed the chemistry in the brain and this caused the mental illness symptoms.

The movement in the United States to legalize marijuana helped me to get some satisfactory answers. I found plenty of articles and research that presented strong evidence that marijuana causes psychosis and loss of IQ in some users. One Swedish physician embarked on a thorough study of nearly 50,000 Swedish military draftees, all surveyed about their drug use. Following up years later, the researcher found that those admitting to using pot frequently as teens were six times more likely to develop schizophrenia than non-pot-smokers. His 1987 paper in *The Lancet* spurred further work, and studies in New Zealand and the Netherlands found comparable associations. A 2004 review of studies on marijuana use, published in *Progress in Neuro-Psychopharmacology*, reported that regular pot-smokers got into motor-vehicle accidents more often than nonusers and were more likely to develop schizophrenia. Some studies, the review noted, also suggested a link between marijuana use and depression. Children of mothers who used pot during pregnancy, other studies suggested, develop neurological problems more often, including memory impairment and reduced ability to process information. [6]

Sharon never used marijuana so this latter study regarding mothers does not apply in that regard except that I believe that Sean did begin using marijuana at an early age and could explain some of the later psychosis. In any event, it seems that there are two things that are certain about marijuana. The first is

8 – OXYCONTIN

that marijuana does not discriminate. It attaches itself to all sorts of different people. The fortunate, unfortunate, happy, sad, educated, wealthy, and the poor are all eligible. The second certainty about marijuana is that whomever it attaches to, marijuana will do damage if it lingers.

My reading on the subject leads me to believe that it is beyond doubt that frequent marijuana use damages the brains of teenagers and young adults. Throughout adolescence and into the mid-20s, the brain continues to develop in ways that are critical for higher order thinking, memory, reasoning, and problem solving. Exposure to drugs during this time has a greater impact on the brain than it does during adulthood.

In the early 30s, marijuana interferes with neural efficiency. In the literature, Psychologists noted the effect of marijuana use during this important developmental period to include cognitive decline, poor attention and memory, and diminished IQ.

> *'It needs to be emphasized that regular cannabis use, which we consider once a week, is not safe and may result in addiction and neurocognitive damage, especially in youth.' Dr Krista Lisdahl, a director of the brain imaging and neuropsychology lab at University of Wisconsin-Milwaukee.*

In a 2012 study of 1037 participants who were followed from birth to age 38 it was found that those who regularly used marijuana lost on average of 5.8 IQ points by the time they reach adulthood. This was compared to those who never

AMEND A BROKEN MIND

regularly used marijuana whose IQ slightly increased by 0.8 IQ points from childhood to adulthood.

Furthermore, brain scans of regular marijuana users show significant structural changes including abnormalities in the brain's gray matter. These abnormalities are associated with reduced cognitive function, increased mood symptoms and poor memory. These changes have been found in users as young as 16 and were not related to major medical conditions, prenatal drug exposure, developmental delays or learning disabilities.[7] Finally, I also read, in a 2004 review of studies on marijuana use published in *Progress in Neuro-Psychopharmacology*, that regular pot-smokers were more likely to develop schizophrenia than non-pot-smokers.[8]

While I was researching the effect of drug use on mental illness, I discovered additionally that early sex abuse can result in later mental illness. Men who were sexually abused as boys share many of the same experiences later in life. The first thing on the list of experiences that applied to Sean was anxiety. He never shared with me that he struggled with severe anxiety which may or may not be caused by stress. However, since I have become his guardian his doctor told me that anxiety is Sean's frequent companion and has been for years.

The second thing on the list was depression. At one hospital stay, Sean was diagnosed as bipolar. Bipolar disorder, also known as manic-depressive illness, is a brain disorder that causes unusual shifts in mood, energy, activity levels, and the

8 – OXYCONTIN

ability to carry out day-to-day tasks (*https://www.nimh.nih.gov* health/topics/bipolar disorder). A third experience common to Sean is that he also has odd obsessive eating habits that change from time to time. One time he decided that he needed to purge his system by eating nothing but rutabagas. When that passed, he became a vegetarian, then he went to high protein diet and ate meat daily, then he became a follower of Jainism and often ate nothing at all.

There are other behaviors that are common to men who were sexually molested as children. Here is a partial list:

- Feeling like "less of a man" or that you no longer have control over your own body.

- Fear of the worst happening and having a sense of a shortened future.

- Concerns or questions about sexual orientation.

- Avoiding people or places that remind you of the assault or abuse.

- Withdrawal from relationships or friendships and an increased sense of isolation.

- Worrying about disclosing for fear of judgment or disbelief.

- Feeling on-edge, being unable to relax, and having difficulty sleeping.

AMEND A BROKEN MIND

- Sense of blame or shame over not being able to stop the assault or abuse, especially if you experienced an erection or ejaculation.

- Withdrawal from relationships or friendships and an increased sense of isolation. [9]

It wasn't until years later after I had been appointed Sean's guardian by the court that one of his doctors told me that it is generally accepted by the psychiatric community that some people are susceptible to psychosis from long term use of marijuana. He felt that this fit Sean's experience. He also shared with me that the molestation of Sean by Joey while I was in Prison was also a big factor in Sean's personality issues today.

Amend a Broken Mind

9 – I Want to Die

Hey, this is Sean again. It seems like it all started to fall apart big time after I had my wisdom teeth out. I had been working at a phone center for a debt recovery company. I spent like all day, every day on the phone calling people asking them to pay back their debts. I was good at it and had been at the job for like about a year when my jaw started hurting bad enough that I finally gave in and had the wisdom teeth taken out.

After the teeth were extracted, the hospital gave me a large bottle of OxyContin with instructions to take one when I felt like the pain was coming on. The day after I was released from the hospital me, my girlfriend Moreen, and our son Chad went to my parent's house for dinner. When my Dad saw the bottle of OxyContin, he was like, "Be careful of those things, Sean. They are very addictive."

It was a typical thing for him to say to me. He thinks I'm a looser and doesn't trust me with anything. But we had a fun time during our visit, and they adore our son Chad who was probably three years old at the time.

The bottle of OxyContin was gone a week later. It was great for the pain in my jaw but also helped with the anxiety that was with me always. It just made me feel all-round better than like usual. I called the doctor to get more but he would not renew the prescription. I was feeling very twitchy and desperately wanted more pills and when I got my check from work, I was looking for the guy who had oxy. I bought all he had. When I got home, Maureen wanted my check to pay the rent. I had nothing to give her having spent it all on the pills, so I told her I was robbed on the way home from work and did not have anything to give her (Laughs). She got all angry and all and started yelling at me. But I was feeling pretty good having taken a few of the pills I bought. Nothing bothered me. I felt like I was made of Teflon.

After a while my jaw stopped hurting. However, I needed more and more pills to keep the anxiety away. I also noticed that I was getting obsessed with the pills. Nothing else seemed to help. So, I talked to my supplier and he showed me how to crush the pills, melt the powder down in a spoon and inject it into my muscle. I like used my shoulder for the injections because the tracks didn't show.

It seemed to work. I did not need as many pills as when I eat them. Nevertheless, the need kept growing until my supplier got busted. So, I went to my parent's bedroom. I knew they would be away and stole some of my mother's pills -- some money too. I got away with this for a while until they confronted me one day. I denied it of course but they went out and bought a lock box for their pills and shit. (Laughs) I was able to get that open with a screwdriver. Then they got a stronger safe. Then they put locks on the doors. It made things more difficult. But I eventually got into that box too. One day my parents confronted me about the drug use. Then Moreen told them I was shooting up the Oxy (laughs).

Amend a Broken Mind

That was funny. They were all being so serious, and my mother was teary eyed. What a show that was. When she tried to talk to me about getting help, I turned it right around on her and told her she was the real drug addict in the family what with all the antidepressants and other pills her doctors had her on. I even called my sisters to tell them Mom was a drug addict.

They didn't know what to say after that. I was high as can be at the time and feeling like I had turned the tables around on them. However, that week I lost my job because my jerky boss told the manager that I was making videos of my key board levitating during the workday. Then, the next week, Moreen was laid off from her job for smoking dope on her breaks.

Moreen and I laughed about the coincidence and commiserated with each other about the idiots at work and how it was not our fault. Moreen even tried to sue her employer for sexual harassment. But that went nowhere.

A short time later we got notice that we were being evicted from our apartment for nonpayment of rent. Moreen was very upset and began screaming and yelling at me just about daily saying that I needed to get a job and support the family. Then I noticed that there were Hispanic individuals hiding in the woods on the other side of the stream behind our apartment. I watched them day and night and began gathering evidence. They were definitely watching our unit. I also got further evidence that Moreen was meeting with them probably giving sexual favors for free drugs.

9 – I Want to Die

One night, before the final date of our eviction, I was alone in the apartment with our son Chad and my Daughter Luna from my first marriage sleeping in the other room. I had scored some pills earlier that day and injected them in my shoulder as usual. As it got dark, I started to see figures everywhere moving around on our back porch and I even heard the doorknob being rattled. I called my mother, my father was traveling on business, and told her what was going on. Of course, she didn't believe me, but she agreed to come over anyway.

The kids woke with all my yelling on the phone and started acting all frightened and everything. There were more dark figures on the back porch, so I called the cops. My Mom arrived a moment earlier than the cops. Wouldn't you know it, when she pulled up, I looked outside and there was like no one around.

I was really upset that mom did not believe me. And the cops acted like I was crazy too. Add to this the kids crying, and I broke down. I couldn't help it. I was like sobbing uncontrollably and told the police that I wanted to die. That was all they needed, they took me to the local hospital and put me under 24-hour suicide watch.

After two or three days I was sent to a treatment center where I stayed for a month until I convinced them that I was okay, and I went back to Moreen and the apartment. She made me make all these promises which I did just to get her off my back. My father came home early from his trip and my Mom

Amend a Broken Mind

had the kids. Our eviction date was a couple days away and we had nowhere to go and no jobs to support ourselves.

We begged my parents to let us stay with them until we could get back on our feet. I told them we would pay them rent as soon as we could. My father said he didn't want to make money from our misfortune but suggested we give them a couple hundred dollars a month to help defer costs. (Laughs) I had no intention of paying them anything but agreed just to get into the house.

Before we moved in with my parents, I knew that Moreen had been secretly meeting on the back porch of our apartment in Laurence with members of a Costa Rican drug gang. She was having sex with them in exchange for booze and drugs. Not only that, but I noticed a platoon of what appeared to be rangers. They were hiding in the woods behind the house. I wondered if they were after me too. They must have found out about the Costa Rican drug gang. I was certain the Rangers had connected me and Moreen with the gang. So, moving in with my parents got her away from Laurence for now.

While we were at my parent's house my parents went away visiting friends in San Diego and my Dad arranged for a contractor to do some work in the upstairs bathroom. And like the second or third night after my parents left, I overheard a radio transmission from the woods. It was the Rangers talking among themselves. They were going to try to enter the house that night. I put couches and beds against the doors on the

9 – I Want to Die

inside to keep them out and began my vigil. I brought my daughter and son upstairs into my Dad's office to hide in case the Rangers got into the house. I had to break the door because it was locked but I had no choice. Nothing happened but in the morning the contractors couldn't get in because of the stuff in front of the doors.

I let the contractors in. They were acting all weird and stuff. I tried to explain to them, but they just started working and ignored me. I overheard one of them calling my father and telling him about what happened with the couches and stuff. My Dad called me later that day and asked me what was going on. I tried to tell him too, but he just said I was imagining things and to let the contractors do their job.

That night I went up into my father's home law office on the 3rd floor of our house so that I could look down into the woods and watch for anyone trying to get into the house. Then I became like convinced that I needed to write a letter to the police and explain what was going on in the neighborhood. I include it here so you can understand what was going on too:

> *Hello, my name is Sean D'Amour. I reside at 36 Lake Street in Byetown, MA. It is my belief that a criminal gang possibly called 2E and possibly originally hailing from either the Dominican Republic or Costa Rica and within the states hailing from Seabrook, NH and Lawrence, MA is*

AMEND A BROKEN MIND

presently carrying out an operation in Byetown with the express purpose of illegally obtaining banking information, social security numbers, and ANY other personal information which might facilitate the creation of fake identities and other identity theft type activities.

It is also likely that data, which could be used in instances of blackmail, is a target for this highly sophisticated group of individuals. I believe they first make friends and develop trusting personal relationships with (likely) young residents of the town thru parties in the area and the local party scenes. One or more members of this group is almost certainly in a secret romantic relationship with most likely more than one of these individuals. After meeting one of the members while we lived for 2 years in Lawrence my girlfriend began a relationship with one of the members of this group. We have a 2-year-old together and I believe that to be her motive in not breaking off our relationship. Also, the neighborhood of Lake and Drescott is ideal for this kind of unusual operation.

There is a spread of small communities which are located around a large area of state and local forest. They move by hiking trail and deer path through the state forests, only occasionally

9 – I WANT TO DIE

needing to touch street or sidewalk, marking safely used trails with sticks which are broken in the form of a letter Y but are laid so the fork part of the Y faces downwards (more on the trails). This form of movement (by trail, at night) allows broad access to a large portion of the Byetown/Orchardland/Radfield area.

They use an abandoned Log Cabin style house on Lake street on the right three houses up. Also, several large abandoned houses which have been illegally rewired for cable and internet all the way from the pole. These are needed as they are in close proximity to their mini network of cables. Unauthorized access to my father's law office, access to tons of personal records, as well as notary equipment, and certainly that kind of access anywhere else.

I've found practice notes for counterfeiting and practicing signatures, etc. I believe the creation of IDs and passports to be at least a means to an end. Identity theft and the acquiring and maxing out of credit cards is likely to be another scam as it seems to be more lucrative than the first.

These individuals have been harassing me mercilessly for months and months now. They steal money, clothing, medication, electronics

AMEND A BROKEN MIND

from me and leave their tags all over the house. I have caught a person that I assume to be one of them sprinting out the back door or jumping from the roof upon my early arrival home on many occasions. I have been onto them for months and months but in the last week this has blown open. I will go into a small amount of detail. Please note this is only touching the surface.

Though I believe this to be a larger gang, possibly 2E (based on the tags I've seen and thoroughly studied) from the Dominican Republic the actual footwork in Byetown/ Orchardland (or any hypothetical area) is carried out by groups of 4-7 males. I have seen a handful of these guys scattering in the headlights of an oncoming car on the side of Lake Street. I believe the target neighborhoods are chosen by geography and a place to leave messages seemingly written in some sort of code.

I should note that from what I've seen, these houses are illegally wired with internet and electricity by actually running cable from the main street lines. I've a decent amount of technical experience and worked at Comcast as well as holding other technical positions as an AV and IT technician at the convention centers

9 – I WANT TO DIE

in Boston. They hang many noticeably low cables. I believe it to be one for each house they are tapping. I'm pretty sure they do phone and internet but at the very least there are internet cables and internet content filtering from their actual physical firewalls located outside of unsuspecting users' houses.

An example of this is the condemned log cabin on Lake Street. It is the third house on the left after the lake heading in the direction of Orchardland and is set back from the road. There has been significant tampering with the cable and sometimes electrical lines of many residences in the neighborhood. Nobody appears to live there, and it has the appearance of being completely abandoned, a red triangle on the front denoting condemned. This house is one of their local regrouping spots and has been rewired with both internet and electricity directly from the lines on the street in front. This also seems to be the place where the hijacked internet is routed for parsing. They have added two separate lines for both internet and cable and sent them to the log cabin. At street level, the tapped electrical line runs out the bottom of the electrical box thru a little black add-on box. I'm pretty sure that above-ground electrical lines do

Amend a Broken Mind

not run underneath 45 yards of leaves, directly on top of the ground under normal circumstances. Directly after the driveway going towards town is the single cable line snaking off the main stem of cables. I've never seen this there before and u can see a coil of cable and other pieces of equipment that would usually not be there. The cable runs thru the air, barely making it and ending clamped to a strange and clearly make-shift contraption that joins both cables and runs them to the house. Thus, rendering free internet and electricity to all within. They have wired a good portion of the neighborhood by using already standing lines and poles for electricity. An example of their lovely lineman's handiwork can be seen on the Lake Street side of the first fork of Millsbury Lane. A line is hanging down to street level.

This is not an official cable line electric line as far as my amateur eye can tell. It's fairly easy to tell where they're running cable due to the large spools of what are probably cat5 cable. This technique would allow them to intercept the signal coming in and heading out of any home that was lucky enough to get in their ambitious paths. It seems to be a reasonable likelihood that they have some sort of connection at a Cable

9 – I Want to Die

company and I have strong reason to believe it to be Comcast (a past employer). With this method there would be a whole variety of methods available for the hacker. The simple keylogger or data interception and sorting would be the obvious choice but I have reason to believe It would even be completely feasible to eavesdrop using the microphone and even camera of an ipad, laptop, desktop, xbox, iphone, android device and even the new Comcast X1 box which, still in Beta Phase, is an easy potential target for this kind of hack and also could easily be used as a honeypot (a spoof of a familiar wireless router that would circumvent encryption). I am tech savvy and know the ins and outs of home networking. I have recently got this virus on all my computers and have had it so many times I can't count. Formatting the hard drive of my pc, mac, and android phone has become a normal Saturday afternoon activity.

I have a couple hypothesis about why this all started and especially why they seem to be focused on me. The reason for the particular angst against me (which seems considerable) is simply my relationship with Maureen. She can talk a serious game and gets a kick out of pitting people against one another. Also, she and I still

Amend a Broken Mind

have an intimate relationship and I'm pretty sure she's broken it off and restarted her relationship with her main squeeze out of the guys multiple times. I have sheets of paper that show Moreen trying to forge signatures and trying to copy script in other people's handwriting as well as what I am fairly certain are gang codes written in her very unique handwriting. There are myriad other incentives for her to be involved with this operation and proofs thereof, but the primary motivation is the payment of her college loans which demand a SIGNIFICANT amount of funds every month. Of which she claims to have none.

I have seen Moreen meet up with a member of this group of men on multiple occasions. I have seen more than six of them at once under cover of night acting as if they on some sort of army mission. I've been personally harassed for months. I've been able to match tags in my house, on notebooks, carved into wood in the house to exactly matching tags outside, on the nearby street from Lake Street. I can identify at least number by name and MOST IMPORTANTLY I'm in possession of what I believe to be multiple sheets of paper which

9 – I Want to Die

contain writing by Moreen and one or more members.

They like to write their correspondences in random pages of books, etc. I have several of these pages which are written in Moreen's handwriting but are not even from a location to which she admits to ever having been. I have multiple items such as rolling papers, flashlight, notebook and more I can't remember off the top of my head, which would certainly have the fingerprints of one of these individuals. In fact, I'd be surprised if the house was not covered in usable prints as I am aware of Juan and perhaps more of his "boys" being in this house on a regular basis.

While I was in my father's office, I became convinced that he was involved in this business that was haunting me. While going through his files I found documents regarding immigration matters between the USA, Costa Rica and the Dominican Republic. I knew the person in the documents. He lived just down the street. This was no coincidence and it really spooked me. Again, I looked outside to see the Rangers in the woods watching the house. I stayed up all night, but the Rangers did not make a move and Juan and his gang were nowhere to be found. They probably also saw the Rangers around the house.

Amend a Broken Mind

The next morning, I took the documents and went to the house of the neighbor down the street to confront him about his and my father's involvement with Costa Rican drug gangs that were in our neighborhood and going after my girlfriend. He acted like he did not know what I was talking about. He even got angry with me for having his private legal documents. His denial and anger really got to me and I told him off, threw the papers at him and ran back home.

When I got home, I looked at my cell phone to check for messages and I realized that I had been hacked. It was subtle. I noticed that my phone was really slow. It was then that I looked some more, and I could see the code moving in from some outside source. My first thought was that the Chinese got into my phone. I was amazed that they could move so fast. I just got the phone a couple days before. My Dad gave me the money. I told him I could not get a job without it and he fell for it (Laughs). He gave me the money to get the phone. But now the phone has been hacked and I can't get it to stop. I told my Dad when he got home from work and of course he did not believe me. So, I showed him. How could he not see the data streaming out of my phone? His comment was, "Sean, why would the Chinese waste time on hacking you?"

Asshole, he never believes me!

Amend a Broken Mind

10 – Decision Time

While Sean was having delusions, paranoia, manic depressive episodes, and going in and out of the hospital, I had been working as a traveling sales manager for the meteorological equipment manufacturer. During an annual job review in 1998, I was told by the company President that he was very pleased with my performance. Hearing this same review year after year from him I felt emboldened and said, "Thank you, but what does the future hold for me at this company? What are my advancement options?"

He replied with an annoyed look on his face, "Nothing, you continue to do what you are doing."

On my own time I had been researching options for where my work experience might lead me in the future. My boss's comment just confirmed that I was on the right track. I accelerated the process of looking for another opportunity at another company with higher responsibility and more pay. After much consideration, asking God for help, talking with men I trusted, and interviews at schools I decided I would go to law school nights. My research showed that people with law degrees and business and sales experience were highly sought after by companies for division management positions.

I began the application process to find a law school to attend and a few acceptances came in the mail. I found one 20 minutes from my home with an evening program and sent in my notice of acceptance along with a check. I was honest about my past and it did not seem to be a problem. However, when I sent in a request for tuition reimbursement to my company the president came into my office and tossed it back with a big red line across it. "This company is not going to pay for you to go to law school," he said and left my office.

Sharon saw the acceptance letters come in the mail. She was waiting for me to say something about it when I came home from work and told her, "Can you believe that jerk boss of mine said the company would not pay for my law school tuition with the tuition reimbursement program?"

She looked at me and asked, "What law school? You didn't say anything to me about this."

I was taken aback a little. Did she not know I was looking into attending law school? I replied, "I got accepted to the Massachusetts School of Law and I start in the fall."

I knew that my being away from home was hard on Sharon and I treated the problem as another challenge to overcome. I read a book about the different ways to look at life and the different parts that make up the whole. One of these that appealed to me was the analogy of life being like a wagon wheel. Each spoke in the wheel was a different area of life: One spoke might be one's social life (how we connect, communicate and get along); another would be our emotional state (how one copes with emotional challenges); still another would be labelled intellectual (one's ability and willingness to be a lifelong learner); then there is the physical state (ones health and ability to make healthy decisions); Spiritual health is another (one's ability to understand their purpose in life); and finally occupational/financial area of our life (one's job fulfillment and balance).

The idea is to look at each area of one's life and determine which areas were being compromised or sacrificed to the others. If the strong areas took too much time and effort from the other areas then the spokes of the wheel would be uneven and the ride on a wagon, held upon such unevenly spoked wheels, would be bumpy and difficult – and (the analogy goes) so would life. The goal is to have balance in one's life and give each spoke equal attention so that the spokes are the same (or nearly the same) length and equally strong.

It was obvious to me that my career spoke was strong at that moment. My health spoke was also in good order from a regular exercise routine and my spiritual spoke was also in reasonably good shape from regular AA meetings and a good prayer life. However, my family relationships were suffering. I tried planning regular dates with just Sharon and this helped some. I figured the best way to help our relationship was to get a job where I did not have to travel. That was why I applied to law school.

However, while I was focusing on this practical analogy of a wagon wheel I forgot to talk to Sharon. Her reaction to my unilateral announcement was not one of enthusiasm. The

10 – DECISION TIME

following letter that she wrote a few days later will give you a taste of what my obsessive search for a smooth wagon wheel cost my relationship with my wife.

The letter read, in part, as follows:

Dear Chad,

It is not that I want to talk about law school (although I do) as much as I want and need to talk about certain dynamics in our relationship of which law school is a part or an example. By that I mean that the way this law school goal or dream has come about has been according to the dynamics of our relationship. One dynamic I have noticed is this: you hurt me, and then you back off and watch me warily to see what my reaction will be. And I, like a compliant, little codependent, Christian girl try to be nice and forgiving (so you won't be unhappy with me! Crazy, huh?) and not show my feelings (because I believe my feelings might displease you or make you uncomfortable) I not only keep quiet about my feelings, I also believe those feelings are not valid.

So, you hurt me and then watch me warily to see if I am going to punish you (and I am dying inside waiting for you to comfort me and show some empathy).

And when you see me sad or angry, you make assumptions that I am trying to punish you. And you

AMEND A BROKEN MIND

back off from me even more. By that I mean you seem to back off even more from wanting to know me and my feelings.

Meanwhile, this is contributing to my feeling powerless, without a voice, lonely and hopeless and tired.

This dynamic reminds me of what happened after we found out about Kate's abuse. Everyone just went on like all was normal. Everything was fine. No one ever tried to comfort us. Remember how it hurt you?

They hurt us and then life went on as if normal. And you start to feel like you are crazy for feeling bad – that there is something wrong with you.

Well, you have hurt me and then you don't seem to understand how your actions have hurt me...

I had no idea what Sharon was going through mentally. I was so wrapped up in my own recovery in AA (meetings 3 – 4 times a week) trying to keep the house fixed up and renovated with more room for the growing family, dealing with the stress on the job, overwhelmed with Sean's behavior, that I really neglected Sharon. We began counselling in a group situation. I think the most useful thing that we got out of our counseling sessions was a tool for talking over difficult issues without hurting each other. It never occurred to me that Sharon wanted to talk about feelings. I saw feelings as problems to fix and would set about fixing them. I was not really very good at

10 – DECISION TIME

identifying or talking about them. In fact, at the time I thought that I had only two feelings – happy and mad. Well, maybe three – frustration too.

Talking, I thought, was highly overrated. But I found out that it was helpful. When I heard from Sharon that my sarcasm and negative comments hurt her, I was able to apologize and even change the way I addressed her. This did take time, of course. As I said, I was very self-absorbed in managing my own chaotic personality and trying to deal with the issues of our children and of work that it was difficult at first to focus on anyone else. In time though things got better. I am forever grateful for Sharon's willingness to hang in there with me.

Since the trauma of the arrest and incarceration, I was not bothered by *le connard* and the out-of-body feelings went away with him. However, I did have a free-floating anxiety that bothered me and a burning obsessive anger that occasionally took over my thoughts. I remember once at work an upper level manager worked out a price for a large piece of equipment by scribbling notes in pencil on the back of a restaurant receipt. I thought it odd at the time, so I put the receipt with pricing penciled on it in a safe place just in case. A month later when the customer placed a large order using the pricing that I gave him, the president of the company went through the roof because the profit on the job was too low.

Amend a Broken Mind

The upper level manager called me to his office and began to berate me in front of the president. I defended myself saying, "But, Mr. Maliakal, you gave me those numbers."

Mr. Maliakal, thinking to call my bluff said, "I never gave you any numbers for any job."

I said, "I kept your notes from the conversation." And ran off to get the receipt from my office.

When I showed it to him, he laughed, ripped it up, and said, "This is very unprofessional, I would never put pricing on the back of a receipt."

I was furious but said nothing more as I was dismissed. That afternoon I could not think about anything but getting back at him. I was so angry I obsessed about jumping him in the parking lot, tying him up and pealing his skin off with a sharp knife.

At that point, I was going regularly to Alcoholics Anonymous, speaking about my experience, strength and hope at hospitals, detox facilities and prisons. I did not drink or take drugs. I did, however, do what I was supposed to do, I called my sponsor. He agreed to meet with me and sympathized with my feelings. He did not help conceive of a plan to get back at the manager. Instead, my sponsor gave me a list of sayings to paste to my dashboard and repeat over and over to help me to break the cycle of obsession. Poems like "The Old Violin":

10 – DECISION TIME

'Twas battered and scarred,
And the auctioneer thought it
hardly worth his while
To waste his time on the old violin,
but he held it up with a smile.

"What am I bid, good people", he cried,
"Who starts the bidding for me?"
"One dollar, one dollar, Do I hear two?"
"Two dollars, who makes it three?"
"Three dollars once, three dollars twice, going for three,"

But, No,
From the room far back a gray bearded man
Came forward and picked up the bow,
Then wiping the dust from the old violin
And tightening up the strings,
He played a melody, pure and sweet
As sweet as the angel sings.

The music ceased and the auctioneer
With a voice that was quiet and low,
Said "What now am I bid for this old violin?"
As he held it aloft with its' bow.

"One thousand, one thousand, Do I hear two?"
"Two thousand, who'll make it three?"
"Three thousand once, three thousand twice,
Going and gone", said he.

Amend a Broken Mind

The audience cheered,
But some of them cried,
"We just don't understand."
"What changed its' worth?"
Swift came the reply.
"The Touch of the Master's hand."

"And many a man with life out of tune
All battered and bruised with sin
Is auctioned cheap to a thoughtless crowd
Much like that old violin

A mess of pottage, a glass of wine,
A game and he travels on.
He is going once, he is going twice,
He is going and almost gone.

But the Master comes,
And the foolish crowd never can quite understand,
The worth of a soul and the change that is wrought
By the Touch of the Master's Hand.'

     - Myra Brooks Welch

Prayers like the Saint Francis prayer:

'Lord, make me an instrument of your peace.
Where there is hatred, let me bring love.
Where there is offense, let me bring pardon.

10 – DECISION TIME

Where there is discord, let me bring union.
Where there is error, let me bring truth.
Where there is doubt, let me bring faith.
Where there is despair, let me bring hope.
Where there is darkness, let me bring your light.
Where there is sadness, let me bring joy.
O Master, let me not seek as much
to be consoled as to console,
to be understood as to understand,
to be loved as to love,
for it is in giving that one receives,
it is in self-forgetting that one finds,
it is in pardoning that one is pardoned,
it is in dying that one is raised to eternal life.'

"And oh, by the way," he said finally, "be sure to get down on your knees and ask God for help,"

I did what he said. I asked God for help and I memorized all the sayings and poems, instead of fixating on how Mr. Maliakal had wronged me, and it worked. I left that company a month or so later to start my quest to become a salesman. Now I was leaving another company to become a lawyer. But, how was I going to pay for this? My buddy Dick from the prison AA program died years ago. But I could hear his voice still telling me, "Get on your knees and ask God for help

AMEND A BROKEN MIND

11 – MEDITATION'S THE ANSWER

Hey, this is Sean. I did pick up something useful during the last hospitalization. We spent a lot of time meditating as a method to calm our inner turmoil. I found it extremely helpful. Sitting quietly, ignoring everything around me, and focusing on my breathing worked. And, unlike all the meds they gave me, there were no side effects.

I was curious so I looked up meditation on the internet. I discovered that what I was doing was part of the Hindu tradition. I also saw that there were all sorts of deities associated with Hinduism. One deity that appealed to me was Vishnu. Vishnu was like the second deity of the Hindu trinity. He is the Preserver. He preserves life by encouraging us to be righteous, truthful, orderly, and principled. He gives the ability to remain at peace in the face of fear or worry. He was often shown with a snake around his neck or underfoot. To me the snake was like the evil and the confusion that seemed to rule my life. In Hinduism it's like when one is good then good things happen in life. When one is bad then bad things happen. This made sense to me. All that was going on was a result of my pride, lust, and self-serving behavior. I wanted to change things in my life, and this seemed like a good path to take.

My parents allowed me to come home after the treatment period was over. I had to agree to take the meds and follow up faithfully with the outpatient plan. I had to take regular blood tests to make sure I wasn't taking Oxy. I was taking four different medications. I know I was taking Lithium for the bi-polar manic symptoms like hyperactivity, rushed speech, poor judgment, reduced need for sleep, aggression, and anger. The Lithium made me feel drowsy, a little dizzy and I developed a twitch. I was also taking Levothyroxine because my thyroid was not producing enough thyroid hormones. I took Suboxone for the opioid addiction. Finally, I was on Lamotrigine for the depressive side of Bi-polar.

Ugh, is all I can say. There is nothing wrong with me. All these drugs are part of the problem. If I could just go live the life of a monk in the woods, I'd be okay. But I agreed to keep on the program, so when I got out, I got a job right away doing sound tech work for a swanky hotel downtown. My Dad went to the men's clothing store and he bought a couple suits for me to wear at work (the hotel required suit and tie).

I did well for a while or until Joey killed himself. I was really, really, really, angry about that. That fucking asshole! He fucked me up royally and then took the easy way out before I could get my ducks in a row. I had been thinking of how I could get back at him. But I did not want to hurt my Dad who seems to have forgiven him. It really pisses me off thinking about how my Dad treated Joey better than he treated me. After all Joey did to me and Kate. I couldn't remember what Joey had done when my Dad first asked me about it, but I have been remembering lately. In nightmares I have seen Joey coming to me and messing with me in bed – sticking his dick in my mouth, trying to fuck me up the ass. I need to stop now. The

Amend a Broken Mind

voices are getting loud again and I'm shaking so much I keep dropping the mic.

(Editor, two days pass)

I'm okay now. I meditated for a while. I was like in the yard under the forsythia bushes. My Dad came out after a while and told me to come in and eat. This news about Joey sort of messed me up in my new job. But, also, my boss felt threatened by me. I was working audio/video support at this swanky downtown hotel. He used to go out the back door and smoke dope while I worked setting up mics. and video equipment. One day the boss was out sick or something, and I had to set up this conference room with a microphone at every seat and a large panel monitor in the front of the room. I had a hard time concentrating and I could not get the mics and video hooked up without major feedback and the hotshots from the company kept ragging on me all the time. I began to shake and get really anxious and the whole day was a big fail.

The boss asked for a letter describing what happened and I wrote a detailed description of the technical problems, failure of equipment, and lack of enough help. I also copied the head office but, in that letter, I told them about my boss smoking dope. Well, the bottom line was, they believed my boss's story which included his claim that I was smoking dope out the back and that was probably why I could not do the job. But I was clean like my weekly drug tests showed.

11 – Meditation's the Answer

I did like to smoke my own rolled tobacco cigarettes out the back of the hotel. The stoop was across the street from St. Francis House and I found myself envying the homeless guys there. They didn't have bosses, girlfriends, or parents telling them what to do. They were like truly free.

As I headed home, all I could think about was what my Dad was going to say when he found out I'd lost another job and how disappointed Moreen was going to be. It was clear to me that the real problem was all the meds I was taking. I congratulated myself for my decision a couple days before to stop taking the Lithium. The Suboxone would be next. I could almost hear Vishnu calling me to trust him. I would meditate all the time and show them all!

As I expected, my Dad was angry. However, this time I thought he was going to cry. He was so sad looking. What the fuck? I've got this! I went to the living room and sat in the meditation pose in front of the fireplace. Moreen sat next to me and tried to talk to me but I refused to answer. My Mom came in and tried but I was determined.

I stayed on the living room floor, silent and not eating for a couple weeks. Then my Dad approached me and said, "Sean, have you stopped taking your medication?"

I looked at him pleading with him to understand, but I could not talk to him. He then asked, "When are you going to eat? You can't keep on like this."

Amend a Broken Mind

I could only shake my head and he replied, "I need you to go with me to the hospital. This is getting dangerous."

As usual, he did not understand me and what I was trying to do. However, this time I was not going to agree to go to the hospital. He, my Mom, and Moreen kept after me for a few days when I finally left the house. I had been communicating with a guy on Craig's List to drive his car to California and when he was ready, I went.

It took a week to get there, but I was finally back in Oakland. I felt like I was coming home. I was thrilled to find out that dope was legal and started smoking it since it was more available than food. I set up a campsite in the Oakland Hills and kept my head down – only going into town every few days to get something to eat.

Cool things were happening when I went into town. I prayed for the people who gave me food or talked kindly to me and I was even able to heal some of them. Unfortunately, I accidentally got caught up in this anarchy rally and ended up in jail. I was there a few weeks when I was taken to court, and the judge released me for lack of evidence.

Then things started happening and I decided to go back home. I promised my Dad I would tow-the-line (as he is fond of saying) if he let me return and he sent me bus fare. I stopped off in Georgia on the way back and hung around on the beach, but they were not friendly to the homeless and I had nothing – no

11 – Meditation's the Answer

money or anything. I tried to cash in the balance of the bus ticket but with no success.

After getting picked up a couple times by men looking for sex, I finally found a peaceful place along a river like about a mile from downtown Fayetteville. I hung out around there occasionally going into town to bum or shoplift. I had a pretty comfortable camp site with stuff I picked from dumpsters or found along the curb. I didn't need much to eat and spent my days meditating. Unfortunately, it started raining and the river rose until it washed everything I had away. It almost got me too (laughs).

I went to a shelter for flood victims at the high school and called my parents. They were frantic to find out where I had been. I guess I was out of contact for three months. I called Moreen who was visiting her parents in Virginia and she agreed to drive down and meet me in Fayetteville. That turned out to be a mistake. When I got to her parent's house on a golf course, I found out that she snuck out at night to meet some guy to smoke dope and have sex. I confronted her and she denied it of course. We got into a big screaming match and her parents told me to leave the house. I mean, come on – I saw what she was doing. It was probably Jose from one of the gangs that followed her out there.

I called my parents who drove down to Virginia and picked me up downtown about six hours later. We drove home and I was feeling really good due to the speed that I took from

AMEND A BROKEN MIND

Moreen's mother and I talked the whole way explaining what happened and the details of what I saw on the golf course.

Once we got home to Byetown, I settled down in the living room in front of the fireplace. I brought sticks and leaves in from the yard to munch on. My Mom got annoyed because she said it looked like I was sitting in a nest with all the leaves and sticks around me (Laughs). She can be really odd sometimes. So, after a few days meditating in the living room, I left and went to stay in a cave in the woods about a mile down the street. I was doing fine eating tree bark and leaves. They were surprisingly good.

After a week or so, my Dad found where I was and talked me into coming home to eat. Once I got home, I decided to stay because it had been snowing and it was very cold outside. I hung around the house in Byetown meditating out in the forsythia bush when the weather permitted. It was an emotionally comfortable place because we used to play "fairy house" in the bushes when we were younger. I felt safe there. Then one day a Byetown police officer and a county sheriff came and put cuffs on me and just took me away. My Dad came out from the house to see me off but did not say anything.

I was taken to the courthouse in Salem and the judge told me I could get a job, go to counseling or go to jail for 90 days. I told her, "I do not want to do any of those things. I am a holy man and need to meditate."

11 – Meditation's the Answer

She seemed hung up on me going to work but I refused to give in, so she sentenced me to 90 days in jail. I don't know what it was all about, but they took me to the county jail. The food was crap and I refused to eat. After 30 days or so they sent me to Bridgewater State Hospital. They restrained me and told me if I did not eat then they would install an intravenous feeding line. So, I ate a vege-burger and some salad. That got them off my back and I sat on the floor and continued to meditate eating only when they insisted.

I was there about a month when they sent me to Tewkesbury State Hospital – something about a commitment for six months. I couldn't drink the water there because it was recycled from the toilets and the food was like nothing I could eat either. The nicer ward workers brought healthy energy bars and nuts in for me to eat and my parents brought a container of white rice with black beans and raw cashews when they came for their weekly visit.

I think I was there because I refused to work or go to the hospital again. Well, I'm still there. I've been at Tewksbury for over a year. They keep promising me that I could go outside or go to a less restrictive place if I would just take a shower, be more friendly to the other patients, eat their food, etc., etc., etc. I do what they say (although I haven't showered since I got here) but nothing happens, and they like change the rules of their game from time to time.

Then I got a letter from my little sister Flo. Here it is in part:

AMEND A BROKEN MIND

Sean:

I love you. I always will - no matter what.

But, I'm angry, hurt. I feel confused and manipulated

I feel like you never really cared about me until I was old enough to be cool and hang out with.

You have a huge effect on People's lives., You're expansive, destructive, and charismatic.

I understand part of what's going on in you because I am bipolar. I don't have delusions like you do, but I think I could. I take care of myself and monitor my moods carefully. I rapid reflux, so I go quickly from depressed to manic to neutral. Stress triggers me. So, I try to limit potential stress causes. I try to have a balanced lifestyle because when I don't, I have bad manic attacks and paranoia.

I don't trust my own feelings., I don't know what emotions are real because they aren't real most of the time. But I still feel very strongly and pour my feelings out in healthy venues like music. Theatre, writing or running.

Honestly, it's extremely important to me because otherwise my mind plays tricks on me and I feel awful.

I've felt really awful about you for a while. I was both relieved and terrified when you went to California.

11 – Meditation's the Answer

Mostly, I was afraid you would get hurt or in trouble and I felt worry for your emotional and mental state. Then when you came back, I felt anger. You did not apologize for or even acknowledge that you ran out on your family, your children and your partner and put us through immense stress and fear all the time you were gone.

I think that you think you had a good reason and were in the right. I think that you don't know how truly awful everything in your life has become.

You have an illness, Sean. You are a normal, average man who is plagued with an illness that affects millions of people around the world, I included. You need to get help before it gets worse and you hurt yourself or someone else.

Mom and Dad can't support you forever. Moreen won't stay with you forever, your children won't want anything to do with you and Katie and I have our lives, problems, and emotional issues to deal with. Please get help.

I hate this but for my own mental and emotional well-being I cannot have anything to do with you until you are seeking help and getting healthy.

I love you always,

Flo

AMEND A BROKEN MIND

That letter at least explained like why my Dad would not give me Flo's address and contact information in NYC when I asked him for it a while ago. However, Flo does not realize that I am the second coming of Christ and I have an obligation to pray for the sinners of this world.

AMEND A BROKEN MIND

12 – LAW SCHOOL

It was 1997 and God answered my prayer again. The answer was a call from one of the country's largest sensor manufactures. I went to an interview, and they offered me a $20,000.00 sign on bonus, offered to pay my law school tuition, offered me a salary that was higher than at my existing company, and I could work from my home. Finally, I was on my way to law school.

I told this story years later at a prison A.A. meeting as an example of how God answers prayer and a prisoner in the audience said *Soto* voice, "Man, this guy's lucky."

There have been too many coincidences for me to believe that it is luck. I immediately resigned from the outside sales job that I had for 17 years and I began to work for the sensor company days while I attended law school evenings. Law school was the most intellectually challenging experience I have ever had.

Jump ahead two and a half years, and I find myself laid off from my job at the sensor company two weeks after I graduated from law school. It was nothing I had done. The company had been purchased by an even bigger company and they wanted to use their own sales force. I determined to use the time during my layoff to study for the bar exam. However, I failed the first time I took it. When I graduated, everyone who knew me assured me that I would have no problem with the Bar Exam.

Unfortunately, I believed them. As a result, I did not take the bar review course offered by the school. I did not practice writing essays. I did not practice multiple choice questions. Predictably, I did not pass the exam.

It was my daughter Katie who told me I had failed. She called me to tell me I received a letter from the Board of Bar Overseers. I said, "Cool, that must be the result of the exam. Open it up Katie and let me know what it says."

She hesitated and said, "I don't think I want to be the one to open this."

I was in the car on the way to the airport to pick up Sharon who was returning from a visit to her mother in the hospital in Arizona. Traffic was awful as usual in the Boston area. And I said, "Come on, Katie, open it. I don't want to wait until I get home to find out if I have passed."

She replied, "I can see what it says through the envelope. I don't want to be the one to tell you what it says."

I realized what she was saying and changed my tone, "Please open it, honey. It is not your fault whatever it says. I won't blame you."

I could hear the rattling of paper tearing and Katie read reluctantly, "We are sorry to inform you that you have not passed the Spring 2001 Massachusetts Bar Exam."

She said, "I'm sorry Daddy."

Amend a Broken Mind

I choked back a sob and replied, "That's okay Katie. It's not your fault."

She signed off quietly and I began to cry. I finally pulled over and wept harder. My mind was reeling. I had no job; the next exam was three months away and results would not be ready for six months. How was I going to support my family for six-months? I felt as hopeless as I had twenty years before when I drove towards the cliff along the river in an aborted suicide attempt. I prayed to myself, "God, what can I do?"

Without warning, clear as can be, I heard a voice say, "Trust me!"

It startled me so much I stopped crying and listened. Wondering if I was losing my mind. It was then that I heard the voice again say, "Trust me!"

I was absolutely certain that God was answering my prayer. The voice did not say, trust in yourself, or trust in Him, or trust in anything else. It said, "Trust Me!"

Six months later, when I had taken the Bar Exam again, I passed. This time I left nothing to chance. I studied hard and trusted God. He provided for us. I did not have to work. I received an unexpected $20,000 bonus check from the company that laid me off. I collected unemployment. And money came in from here and there – just enough to meet the financial needs without us having to use up our retirement savings.

12 – LAW SCHOOL

A few weeks after I passed the Bar, I received an invitation from the Massachusetts Board of Bar Overseers to attend one of their board meetings. On the way in I did what I knew Dick would tell me to do. I asked God for help.

The board chair wanted to know about my Felony conviction back in 1980. He asked, "Why should we allow you to practice law in the Commonwealth of Massachusetts with a felony conviction? Tell us about the circumstances of your arrest and incarceration."

I replied as honestly and openly as I could, "I was an alcoholic. I acted out when I drank. Since the arrest twenty years ago I have not had a single drink and I have not been arrested again. I speak regularly at Alcoholic Anonymous meetings in hospitals, prisons, and detoxes sharing my experience strength and hope with other alcoholics."

He looked around and the board seemed to reach a silent agreement. "Very well," he said. "We will approve your membership application to the bar. Congratulations! But, make sure you don't start drinking again!"

I was sworn into the Massachusetts Bar at Faneuil Hall in Boston by a justice of the Massachusetts Supreme Court. Then, I went to the new Federal Courthouse on the bay in South Boston and was sworn into the Federal Bar by a Federal District Judge. Next, I rented some space down the street from the courthouse in Salem, Massachusetts and began to practice law.

Amend a Broken Mind

After a few weeks of taking whatever client walked in off the street (I represented a witch, a couple slip and falls, an adverse possession, child/parent cases, etc.), and in an effort to attract business law clients, I travelled to a NYC trade show. Once there, I walked around the hall handing out my *Curricular vitae* to the companies in the various booths. At one booth I began talking to the President and owner of a small industrial sensor company in Connecticut. We had lunch together and over the following months he began to pass legal work on to me. After a year of doing various legal chores for them I got to know the company well. Consequently, I spoke to the President about how I could double his business in five years if he would hire me full time.

Subsequently, he gave me a chance. It was Thanksgiving time in 2002 and for the next few years I worked out of my home in Massachusetts seeking new business for the sensor company until the company grew such that it became necessary for me to move to Connecticut. Business continued to grow as I turned the focus of the company away from designing and manufacturing industrial sensors toward designing and manufacturing medical sensors. Business doubled and we built a new building. Sales and profits doubled again, and I was given an ownership position in the company.

Also, during this post law school period, I was able to build an 18-foot sailboat out of wood. It was a custom design that I had in mind for years. With the help of Chuck, a boat builder friend of my son, we put my design on paper and built it in four

12 – LAW SCHOOL

months. It was a real beauty. I painted the hull white and the deck sea green. We took her to the wooden boat show in Mystic Sea Port, Mystic, CT. After the show the Wooden Boat Magazine from Brooklyn, Maine asked me if they could write an article on the boat that I christened the Marian Gray. We called the design Ipswich Bay 18.

I was invited to sail the Marian Gray at a regatta of small wooden boats at the wooden boat school campus in Brooklyn, Maine on the bay across from Deer Island. I went with Chuck to the regatta that weekend. It was a lot of fun with 50 small wooden boats sailed by their builders over the period of four days sailing without motor power from island to island in the Deer Island archipelago.

On the third day of the regatta I was sailing with an older man who wanted to try a different boat while Chuck went on to try another boat also. It was a very calm day and the fleet rowed along in the beautiful surroundings. Around noon time I noticed out toward the opening of the bay a large bank of fog heading our way. No one was alarmed because it was so calm, and we were 50 or so boats bunched close together. We were so close to each other that conversations were going on all around me. It had a calming effect that caused me to be less alarmed of the fog bank than I think I would have been if I was alone on the boat in the open bay.

This part of the bay was 800 feet deep and the water was below 40 degrees Fahrenheit. The air was warm and still until

AMEND A BROKEN MIND

the fog enveloped us. Then air temperature dropped, and the wind picked up suddenly from dead calm to about 20 knots. The man who was with me, I soon found out, was not a sailor but was there with a friend and knew nothing about handling small boats.

I asked him to take the tiller and keep the Marian Gray headed into the wind while I shortened sail. He took the tiller and sat on the leeward side of the boat as he turned into the wind. Before we could come up into the wind, he turned the tiller the other way and the sails filled again, and we flipped total turtle. With our rudder and center board pointing straight at the sky and our mast pointing straight to the bottom of the ocean.

The first thing I realized was that the water was numbing cold; second, I was under the boat tangled in the lines and sail; and third, I could not free myself. The more I moved the more tangled I got. It was odd because, while I was trapped under the boat, I was calm and remember thinking, "This is one scenario from which I will not to be able to escape."

As I was stuck under the boat holding my breath, I thought of Sharon shopping in Brooklyn, Maine while I was in the cold waters of Eggemoggin Reach. I thought of my children and grandchildren. I thought of Dick and I prayed, "Please, God. Don't let me die here – not like this."

The next moment I reached out, felt the gunwale of the boat and pulled myself out from under. I took a big, grateful breath

12 – LAW SCHOOL

of air and tried three times to pull myself onto the overturned hull of the boat. To my dismay the hull was very slippery, and I could not reach the rudder to hang onto and pull myself up. By this time, I was shivering uncontrollably. Then I realized I had a length of line in my hand that was three feet long. To this day I have no recollection of grabbing it. Nevertheless, I took each end in a hand and flicked it over the rudder. I then pulled myself up out of the water. I looked around and saw my crew floating in the water hanging onto a life jacket a few feet from the overturned hull. I flicked the line to him. He clutched it and I pulled him up out of the frigid water onto the overturned hull of the Marian Gray.

The fog was still pea soup thick, but the wind had died down. Fortunately, other regatta boats were nearby, and we got help quickly. I got a change of clothes and my crew sat in the bottom of the rescue boat with a towel around his shoulders shivering violently.

I got help from another sailor who had a grapple on the end of a long line, and we righted the Marian Gray. I followed him to shore rowing the Marian Gray to the beach on a nearby island and regrouped. After I warmed up a little and calmed down a lot I rowed back to the starting point where Sharon was waiting for me with tears in her eyes. News traveled fast.

I will not try to kid you and tell you that the next day I was right back out there. The damage to the boat was enough to keep me on shore doing repairs. Furthermore, I was feeling

AMEND A BROKEN MIND

unsure of myself – unsure enough that I did not go out sailing again the rest of that summer. Even though Chuck and I did some capsize drills on the local lake, my confidence in my sailing abilities would take a while to recover from that afternoon.

A few years after the sailing accident, disaster struck at work. The two original owners got divorced. Bam! Half of their assets were converted into debt to pay off their ex-wives. This happened in the summer of 2015 and they naturally turned to me to increase the business faster. My sales goal was doubled to a level that was impossible to meet without purchasing a company with an existing incremental business. Unfortunately, the other two owner's debt was now the company's debt and there was no money for purchasing a company or hiring more people. Furthermore, they both began to spend less time in the office and more time with their young girlfriends. The situation in the office became untenable. I found myself managing production, scheduling engineering, working on Marketing, organizing and attending trade shows, answering all incoming sales calls, resolving legal issues and handling negotiations for new and renewed contracts.

On top of the difficulties at work, Sharon developed breast cancer and began weekly treatments that wiped her out emotionally and made her physically ill. Sean was acting up at our house in Byetown while we were in Connecticut trying to grow the business so that the owners could get their assets back.

12 – LAW SCHOOL

In time, Sean lost custody of his daughter Luna because of his failure to pay child support and because of the chaos at home. Moreen and he were fighting all the time often getting the police involved. Furthermore, Moreen had been stopped by the police for a routine traffic violation. During the stop the officer noticed she was glassy eyed and found marijuana on her possession. Fortunately, my grandson was not with her at the time. However, child services came to my house where Sean, Moreen and our grandson Chad were living to see what the home situation was.

In 2012 my nephew Joey committed suicide by hanging himself on a tree in the woods near his house. Joey had recently been arrested for indecent exposure to a young girl. He was looking at more jail time because he was out of jail on parole when he exposed himself. Since the time he had molested Kate and Sean he had been in and out of jail for various sexual crimes. One of which involved his own two daughters. That incident resulted in a divorce and court order to have no contact with his ex-wife and children. His legal costs were exorbitant, and he had trouble holding a job. At one point he came to me looking for free legal help. I demurred.

Although I had helped other family members get out of various legal messes I could not afford to get involved with Joey's legal issues. He wanted me to fight his listing on the public sex offender web page and defend him against some of the outstanding charges. I told him I could not get involved with his legal issues. Unknown to Joey, Sean was talking about suing him for what he had done to him when Sean was a child.

Sean's reaction to the news of Joey's suicide was significant. He was very angry and accused me of treating Joey better than I treated him. One day when Sean was particularly agitated, he began angrily speaking to me about my relationship with Joey. With anger flashing in his eyes Sean said, "You never did anything to Joey after you found out about what he did to me and Kate. You went on like nothing happened. You care about him more than you care about me!"

I reminded Sean that Joey did jail time, that I refused to help Joey with his legal problems, and that I tried numerous times to get Sean to talk to psychiatrists all of whom he said were idiots. I also reminded Sean that he told me repeatedly that he could not remember anything between him and Joey. Nothing I said got through to Sean. This was in the year 2013 and, unknown to me, Sean had quit another job and had been slowly cutting back on his medication again.

It was just before Christmas that year when Sharon and I came home from Connecticut for the holiday. There were a couple feet of snow on the ground and temperatures were below freezing with a strong wind bringing the chill factor to zero degrees Fahrenheit. When we arrived at Bytown we found the driveway had not been shoveled. I had to clear out a space to park the car and a path to get to the house. We wondered why the Christmas tree that we had set up and decorated earlier was

12 – LAW SCHOOL

outside in the snow. Inside the house there was a smell of garbage, the sink was full of dirty dishes, all the lights were off, and all the Christmas decorations had been removed.

We found Moreen in the living room with the shades drawn, lights off, and drunk. Our Grandson Chad, my namesake, was playing with toys on the floor in the dining room. Sean was also there. He was delusional, paranoid and agitated. I said to Sean, "It's happening again."

He said, "What's happening?"

"You are regressing into delusions and paranoia."

He sneered at me, "As usual Dad, you are exaggerating. I have stopped taking the Suboxone because I don't need it anymore."

I could see that he was wild eyed and wired up. "When was the last time you slept?" I asked.

"Oh, I don't need to sleep, and I don't need medication. Krishna is my guide."

Regrettably, I have become familiar with the names and side effects of the various medications used to help Bipolar Disorder, Schizophrenia, and drug addiction. Suboxone is known as a "blockbuster" medication with the potential to reduce symptoms of opiate addiction and withdrawal. Suboxone was prescribed to help with Sean's opioid addiction. One of Sean's previous hospitalizations was preceded by using

Amend a Broken Mind

Oxycontin crushed, melted in a spoon with a flame, and injected into his shoulder muscle.

He also said, "I stopped taking the lithium a few weeks ago."

Lithium Carbonate is used to treat manic-depressive disorder (bipolar). It works to stabilize the mood and reduce extremes in behavior by restoring the balance of certain natural substances (neurotransmitters) in the brain. Side effects that Sean has complained about in the past are drowsiness, dry mouth, weight gain, and mildly shaking hands. However, it did a good job of stabilizing Sean's moods.

"I stopped taking the Risperdal a month ago." He continued. "And I haven't felt this good in a long time."

Risperdal is an antipsychotic medication. Side effects that Sean experienced were dry tongue, weight gain and diarrhea.

By this time, after all these years, hospitalizations, Sharon's cancer, the frustration at work, I was feeling very discouraged. My old thoughts surfaced with my growing discouragement, "I can't continue to live like this." I thought. "Why can't I just die?"

I hadn't felt such despair since before I was arrested 35 years ago. However, I was able to shake the feeling off and said, "Sean, you need to go to the hospital, or you need to leave this house."

12 – LAW SCHOOL

He sneered again, "Why don't you leave if you don't like it here?"

Now I was getting angry. I said, "Don't mock me. Look at the situation here. You have lost custody of Luna. Little Chad is traumatized by the screaming and fighting, police are visiting once a week, child services is visiting because of complaints, you are not working, Maureen isn't working, I cannot continue to support your bad decisions. You need to leave or go to the hospital."

He began to mock me again, accusing me of all sorts of things. In the hour that followed conditions intensified. I found a bag of vodka nips hidden in the bathroom. Then I noticed that money had been taken from the dresser in my bedroom. We had installed heavy duty locks on our bedroom and on my office doors recently because things were disappearing from both places when we were otherwise engaged. The heavy-duty locks were necessary because the regular bedroom and office locks had been broken while we were away from the house at the doctor, shopping, or in Connecticut. However, this day, Sharon had left the bedroom open because we were both at home.

My blood was beginning to boil. I felt manipulated by Sean. When he returned home from the last hospital stay, he promised me that he would stay on his medication. He promised me he would not bring alcohol and street drugs into the house. He promised he would work to support his family and pay child support. Now he had broken every promise and he was mocking

AMEND A BROKEN MIND

me and accusing me of assaulting him because I was following him around the house telling him I would call the police if he did not either go to the hospital or leave the house.

Next thing I knew, there was a cruiser out in-front of the house and two police officers knocking at our door. Sean ran to the door and, pointing to me he said, "My father is assaulting me!"

He took the officers upstairs and showed them the door to his bedroom that he had broken the other day by slamming it. He showed them a picture that had fallen to the floor in his bedroom when he slammed the door and told them I broke it in anger.

They looked at me and I said, "He is not taking his medication and I am trying to get him to the hospital or to leave the house because he is frightening the children and making our lives unbearable."

We were downstairs answering the police officer's questions when I lost it and started weeping. Sean came up to me and gave me a hug. One of the officers said, "That is what I like to see. I think we can go now."

After they left Sean said to me, "I know what the right thing to do is, but I am afraid to do it."

I answered, "Your mother and I will drive you to the hospital, then."

12 – LAW SCHOOL

"No", he replied, "The right thing is for me to leave."

I was confused, "Wait a minute. The right thing is to go to the hospital and get treatment."

"No, there is nothing wrong with me. I am going to leave. I should have done this a long time ago."

Sean went to his room, got a backpack and put his iPad in it along with charger and a few clothes, hugged Sharon and me, and left without saying good-by to Maureen or little Chad.

The quiet was eerie after he left. We were all exhausted. Sharon and I lay down in our bedroom and napped. When we woke, we went to the grocery to get something for dinner. I felt like I was walking in a fog – going through the motions of living.

We did not hear from him for weeks. Our imagination went wild. Was he kidnapped, lost, passed out on the side of the road, or dead somewhere? It was torture for us. Sharon and I went to the local police and tried to file a missing person request. They told us that he was an adult and could do whatever he wanted to do. Therefore, a missing person report was not applicable. However, Sharon, God bless her, started crying, told them about the hospitalizations, and how he had stopped taking his medication. Finally, the officer agreed to file the report.

The police were able to track him to Oakland, CA when we lost track of him again until he called collect from the California Department of Correction. I took the call, "Dad, how are you?"

he asked. "I got picked up in a sweep by the police during an anarchy riot. They are holding me at the jail in a cell with a bunch of others."

"What were you doing in a riot?" I asked.

"I wasn't in the riot," he snapped back. "I just came down from my campsite in the hills when I got picked up by the police. I get out in a couple days. I saw a lawyer and he said there was no problem getting released. I just wanted to let you know I was all right."

When he got off the line I talked with Sharon and we went online to find the mental health department in Oakland Department of Correction. We called and talked to a woman who took our information about Sean's history. She assured us that the Mental Health Division would get involved. She also let us know about a web site where we could follow his case.

We spent four days anxiously checking the web site and waiting to find out what would happen to Sean. I'm not sure which was worse, having him with us acting out or having him 3000 miles away in jail. However, when he was released, he called me and asked for a bus ticket home. I finally relented and bought a nonrefundable ticket from Greyhound Bus lines and he headed home – or so he claimed.

We did not hear from Sean for a couple of months. The bus company could only tell us he got on the bus. They had no knowledge of how far he went or where he was. Then, out of

12 – LAW SCHOOL

the blue it seemed, an officer contacted Sharon and told her that Sean had been seen in Savannah, Georgia. A local police officer had stopped him as he walked along the road. When asked who he was Sean answered truthfully. When asked where he was going, he said, "I'm taking a walk down the coast."

The officer replied, "Well, I guess there's no law against that. But call your parents."

Sean called my cell phone from someone else's phone a week later. I didn't recognize the number but answered anyway. "Hey Dad," he said, "I'm in Georgia (Laughs). I need to get another ticket to get home."

I asked, "Where are you planning to stay? You cannot come back here."

He replied, "Erin said I could stay with him for a while."

I repeated with emphasis, "You cannot stay here at the house. You need to go to the hospital. Nothing has changed since you left."

He responded, "There is nothing wrong with me. Erin will let me stay with him."

We agreed that Sean would call me back tomorrow and hung up the phone. I immediately called Erin. Erin was a close childhood friend of Sean's. He lived in Western Mass and when I called him, Erin told me, "I told Sean that he could not stay with me. I have friends visiting. There is too much going on."

"Sean said you were going to let him stay with you."

"No, I told him he could not stay with me. Why don't you let him stay with you? He's your son."

I told Erin what has been going on with Sean and he did not believe me. He said, "I've talked with Sean lately, he said that Maureen was the problem. That she was cheating on him with one of the neighbors. He claimed to have found a condom on the floor in her bedroom. She was crazy too. He claimed that Moreen was possessed."

"He thinks there are rangers in the woods behind us." I said. "He also thinks Moreen has been having sex with the men in the neighborhood across the street. Moreen is not doing what Sean claims she is doing."

Erin started to believe what I was saying. He offered to pay for half of the bus ticket. I said, "You do not understand, he cannot come back here. He has terrorized his children with his delusions and paranoia. He is making our life miserable. He needs to go to the hospital, but he refuses to go."

This discussion went around and around until I agreed to pay half of the ticket. I realized that we could not influence Sean at all if he was not with us. I used my credit card to pay for it and Erin promised to send me a check to reimburse me. I still have not seen the check. Nevertheless, Sean got on the bus and

12 – LAW SCHOOL

headed East from Georgia. Unknown to me, Sean and Moreen were talking with each other and agreed among themselves that Sean would meet her at her parent's house in Virginia. Moreen left suddenly to visit her parents. A week went by and we got calls from Moreen, Sean, Moreen's brother in law, and her parents.

Apparently, Sean arranged for Moreen to pick him up. Also, he had scored some methamphetamines along the way. Consequently, he was so manic that he had not slept in days. When he finally called to tell me, he was with Moreen at her parent's house, he tried to convince me that Moreen was meeting men at night in the golf course alongside Moreen's parent's home. When I talked to Moreen she denied Sean's story about meeting the men on the golf course, adding that Sean was on drugs again.

Moreen's parents said Sean had to leave. He was disrupting their life. Moreen's brother-in-law called me and told me that Sean was telling wild stories and causing Moreen's parents health to suffer. I did my best to explain that Sean was off his medication and needed to go to the hospital.

Sean called again to say, "Dad, they are telling me to leave. No one believes me. But I've seen Moreen out there on the golf course having sex with random men. They won't give me any money. What am I supposed to do?"

Our conversation was interrupted by the arrival of the police to Moreen's parents' house and ended as Sean was escorted out

AMEND A BROKEN MIND

of the house by the police. They took Sean downtown and left him at a hotel. Then I got a call from Moreen. She was very upset. She cried over the phone promising me that the things he accused her of never happened and she was very concerned for Sean. He had no money and was homeless in downtown Alexandria. I asked her to text me the hotel information. I then asked her to go to him and tell him to wait there at the hotel. Sharon and I would drive down that day and pick Sean up. Yes, we would bring him home.

Sharon and I drove to Virginia on August 3, 2014 – our 40th wedding anniversary to pick up Sean. As Sharon cancelled our plans for dinner and a show that evening, I was on the phone with the hotel in which Sean was hole up. I made reservations and asked if Sean could hang out there while we drove down to Alexandria.

It took us seven hours to get to Sean. When we checked into our room Sean was manic and he talked nonstop while we lay down to rest. It became clear to us by-and-by that he would not let us sleep. We finally looked at each other and I said, "Come on, Sean. Let's go home."

We got in the car and started back to Byetown. We stopped a few times for coffee and bathroom breaks. Sean talked nonstop the whole way. He told the story of Moreen's cheating in extreme detail. He said, "She snuck out of the house at 1:00 am and took her parents dog on a leash to make it look like she was walking the dog. But I followed her as it started to rain. She

12 – LAW SCHOOL

crossed the 9th hole and walked to the trees between holes on the golf course. I could see a shadow approach her from the other side of the course. Moreen looked around and I jumped into a sand trap..."

His story went on for the seven plus hours of our return trip. It changed a little with each telling. Details were added and embellished in support of his scenario.

After we got back from Virginia, Sean continued to abuse drugs and continued to claim that there was nothing wrong with him. I confronted him numerous times and his mocking, stealing, paranoia, and delusions continued to get worse. He talked a lot about living in the woods nearby. Then he got a job at a farm a few miles away. He worked there for a month while he lived in the woods. Then he began a new delusion. He claimed he could talk to the cows. "They are holy," he claimed. "They should be worshiped not held in a pen for their milk".

He also told me that the farm was taking truckloads of trash, hazardous waste, refrigerators, stoves and dropping it all on the farm fields. This sort of disparaging talk about his employer often preceded Sean either getting fired or quitting. I was emotionally exhausted! I thought about what Dick would say, "Did you get down on your knees and ask God for help?"

I had by this time come to believe in God's ability and willingness to answer prayer, so it was easier to ask for help than it was when Dick first made the suggestion. That evening Sharon and I prayed for our children and grandchildren, her health, my job situation, and thanked God for all the answers in the past. The next day I got a call from Kevin Contrell. Kevin was a Business Development Manager for a local rep firm. The firm was not officially one of our manufacturers reps. But Kevin and I had collaborated in the past to get some business in the semiconductor industry that was very profitable.

He asked if we could get together for lunch. We met at a local sandwich shop and talked about business opportunities. Then he said to me, "Medical Sensors is a company that I have a great deal of respect for and I am at a point in my career that I am looking to begin a new challenge."

I explained the difficulties that I was facing at the company and said, "Would you be interested in my job?"

He responded immediately, "Yes!"

I looked at his resume and told him, "I will talk to the President and tell him that I wanted to retire, and that I think you would be the right guy for the job."

That is how, at 66 years old and after 15 years with Medical Sensors I retired. We hired Kevin and I worked with him for two years until the owners came up with enough money to buy me out. Then I sold my house in Connecticut and moved back to Byetown in 2017.

While all this was going on, Sharon was undergoing cancer treatments, losing her hair, getting weaker and weaker, and Sean was getting sicker and sicker. These personal issues were

12 – LAW SCHOOL

getting increasingly tough to ignore while I was at work in Connecticut. They made it difficult for me to concentrate on my job and made it difficult for me to do the things that were necessary to do daily. But now I was at home all the time and able to focus on helping where I could.

Sean came around to our house every now and then and would sit in the living room meditating. He refused to talk to us. I was not surprised when it became clear after a while that he was no longer working at the farm. During the day when he was with us, he would go into the yard at our house and collect branches. He would bring them into the house and make a nest in which he sat in the lotus position with his hands off to the either side making the okay sign. As he sat, he would chew on the bark and eat the leaves that were scattered around him in a circle. We occasionally got him to eat some plain rice but that was rare.

After a few weeks of this I tried to get him back into the hospital without any luck. All I could think of was how we sat around the table 25 years ago and sang the song, "Sittin' in my cat box, contemplatin' my navel." We had come full circle. Only now it was my son who was ignoring his children, girlfriend, and work sitting in my living room contemplating his navel. And I was constantly running over again and again in my mind how I could have been a better father and save my son from all this awful confusion, drug addiction, and paranoia.

Amend a Broken Mind

13 – Homeless

Winter 2016 was approaching, and Sean would go into the woods for days at a time. He would usually leave us when I started bothering him about going to the hospital or when I told him his daughter was coming over to visit. I did not know where he was going but when Christmas arrived, he left again without telling us where he was going. This at least allowed us to celebrate Christmas as we would like without Sean tearing down the decorations and throwing out the tree.

At this time, I noticed that there was a box with winter clothes at the entrance to the woods down the street from our house. The sign on the box said, "For the homeless man." These woods are extensive, and I still had no clue where in the woods Sean went, he wasn't at our house. I figured the box, located at a trail head, could have been placed by neighbors concerned that Sean was not dressed for the weather. That is also where I figured he entered the woods. But there are miles of trails in this area. New Year's Eve rolled around. The temperatures were in the low 20s. It was snowing. A couple feet of snow accumulated, and Sean did not come home. Sharon and I were so worried that we walked into the woods with flashlights, on New Year's Eve, calling for Sean and looking for footprints or evidence of his passing. We were frantic.

The last time he left the house he was wearing sneakers, no socks, cotton slacks, and a jersey. We had the picture in our minds of Sean, laying in the snow, freezing to death. He hadn't eaten in days and it was cold and windy. Sharon and I continued to look unsuccessfully for Sean until the batteries in our flashlights began to fail.

The next day, New Year's Day, after a sleepless night, I put on my cross-country skis and went into the woods at dawn to look for Sean at the spot down the street where I had seen the homeless man box. Hours later I found him sitting lotus position on a bed of pine beaus in the mouth of a cave.

Sean saw me first and called out, "Ha, Dad, what brings you here?"

"Aren't you cold and hungry?" I called. "Why don't you come home?"

He said, "Maybe I will."

These are the first words I had heard from him in a while. I didn't know what to do other than turn around, go back to the house, and hope that he would come home.

Then I thought of Dick from back in my early days of sobriety. What would he say? He would ask, "Did you get down on your knees and ask God for help?"

Well, when I got home, I did get down on my knees and ask God for help. My prayer was for God to reveal a way to get Sean back into the hospital. None of the governmental agencies would act without Sean's approval. After all, they reminded me often enough, there is no law against being crazy. It did occur to me though, that there is a law against not paying child support.

The next day I woke with an idea that I thought might work. I contacted Connie, Sean's first wife, and told her what was happening with Sean, and asked her to file a complaint in probate court for nonpayment of child support. Sean had not paid anything in a couple years by this point.

Instead of filing the complaint Connie came to our house, walked into the living room where Sean was sitting in his nest and screamed at him. She called him names like manipulator, fucking loser, phony. She then tried to get him to sign papers allowing her to change their daughter's name to Connie's new married name. When he just sat there and refused to look at Connie, she punched him in the face called him a poor excuse for a man and a father and came out into the kitchen where Sharon and I were waiting. Connie then began yelling at us calling me a coward because I didn't tell her Sean was back from his wanderings. She called Connie a passive, useless old woman. She told me to, "Wipe the puki smirk off your face," and left our house.

Our heads were spinning. Sean was in the living room crying. Sharon and I were stunned. It took her a few weeks of patient cajoling. But, by and by, Connie did as I asked. A notice to Sean from the court for a hearing on her complaint for nonpayment of child support finally arrived at our house.

13 – HOMELESS

When I showed Sean the letter from the court, he refused to look at it. He refused to talk about it. He refused to go to court. The result, when he did not show up at court, was that a warrant for contempt of court was issued for his arrest.

Instead of hanging around waiting to be picked up by the Sheriff he left the house. It was February 2016, and cold and snowy outside but like before he left wearing only a cotton shirt, cotton slacks, sneakers, and a backpack that I had given him last Christmas. He called a few times from Boston complaining that he was cold and had nowhere to go. I offered to come pick him up and take him to the hospital. He responded that he had prayed for some people in a Dunkin Donuts for healing and they were healed. He said, "I think God has something special planned for me."

I gave him the number and address of a NAMI (National Alliance on Mental Illness) drop-in center where he could get some food and shelter if he did not want to go to the hospital with me. However, after that we did not hear from him for six months. Sharon and I feared the worst. We filed another missing person report with the police, and they found him again in Georgia. He walked there this time.

I read a disturbing story of a young woman with Sean's diagnosis who starved to death in a summer camp in Maine after she was released from a New Hampshire mental hospital. Her family was not notified. At the time of her release, she was delusional and refusing medication for her psychosis. She

Amend a Broken Mind

eventually wandered into an abandoned farmhouse where she lived unnoticed for four months before dying of starvation. She left behind a diary describing her survival eating apples, melted snow and reading books during a severe New England winter. Her body was found in the spring by the owners of the farmhouse. This scenario was hauntingly familiar to our fears for Sean.

He returned home from his wanderings this time in the summer of 2017. When he returned home the delusions and paranoia continued. However, he had been able to stop taking the opiates and claimed he was not taking any drugs. Furthermore, he was passive and there were no angry outbursts. However, now he thought he was the second coming of Jesus Christ, able to heal with a touch. He returned to his place in the living room sitting lotus position, meditating all day, and eating bark from twigs he collected in the yard. Finally, after him refusing to go to the hospital and not eating real food I called the Sheriff. I asked if the warrant was still out there for nonpayment of child support. When the sheriff said yes, I told him Sean was at my house in Byetown.

The Sheriff came over with a Byetown police officer and they took him to the courthouse. Sharon was babysitting our grandchildren, so I went alone to the courthouse for the hearing. The court room was emptied, and Sean was brought in. He looked like hell. His hair was long and tangled, his beard was unkempt as well. He was wearing the same clothes he had on

13 – HOMELESS

when he left my house. He had not showered since he got back from his walk to Georgia.

After establishing that Sean gave the Sheriff and police officer no resistance during the arrest, the judge asked me to introduce myself for the record and said, "Mr. D'Amour, do you have anything to say?"

I said, "Yes, your honor. This past New Year's Eve at midnight Sean's mother and I looked for him in the woods until our flashlights went out. He had left the house a couple days earlier in sneakers, cotton slacks, and jersey and headed for the woods. There were a couple of feet of snow on the ground and the temperature was in the low 20s. We expected him back and finally went looking for him when he did not show up New Year's Eve. We did not find him. The next morning, I went looking further into the woods on cross country skis and found him a couple miles from our house sitting in a cave. I told him to come home before he froze to death. We have been trying to get him into the hospital for a year now, but he says there is nothing wrong with him. Just look at him. He is very sick now. He needs to go to the hospital not to jail. I went to the court psychiatrist in Haverhill and she told me there was nothing she could do for me unless he agreed. She said to me that there is no law against being crazy."

"I'm not crazy." Sean said out loud.

I continued, "He refused to go to the hospital, I can't have him in the house because he has called the police on me and he has traumatized the children, but I can't in good conscious just leave him to die of exposure or starvation in the woods."

The judge thanked me, looked at Sean and gave him three choices; he could go to jail for 90 days; he could get a job; or he could go to the hospital. He responded quietly, stuttering a little and said, "I don't want any of those things. I am not sick. I'm practicing my religion."

The judge gave Sean the choices again and when he repeated that he did not want any of them she said, "You leave me no other choice but to sentence you to 90 days in Middleton jail."

After they took Sean away, I went down to the Clerk's office to get a copy of the judgment. While I was waiting there, the arresting deputy Sheriff came up to me and told me, "In a couple days call the jail and ask to talk to the mental health department there. Let them know about your son. The judge will probably call for an evaluation, but it would not hurt to call them yourself."

I was so used to officials telling me they were sorry, but they could not talk to me because of the HIPAA law that I asked, "Will they talk to me?"

He said, "He is in jail now and all that happens is public so, yes they will talk to you."

The HIPAA, Health Insurance Portability and Accountability Act, has as a major goal (according to the Department of Health and Human services):

13 – HOMELESS

"to assure that individuals' health information is properly protected while allowing the flow of health information needed to provide and promote high quality health care and to protect the public's health and wellbeing. The Rule strikes a balance that permits important uses of information, while protecting the privacy of people who seek care and healing. Given that the health care marketplace is diverse, the Rule is designed to be flexible and comprehensive to cover the variety of uses and disclosures that need to be addressed."

There are hundreds of ways that HIPAA Rules can be violated, although the most common HIPAA violations are impermissible disclosures of protected health information. The Rule requires appropriate safeguards to protect the privacy of personal health information and sets limits and conditions on the uses and disclosures that may be made of such information without patient authorization. The Rule also gives patients the right to examine and obtain a copy of their health records, and to request corrections.

Civil penalties for individuals with control of patient information can be large. The law calls for seven figure dollar penalties for repeat violations during the same calendar year. Lower penalties are in the tens of thousands of dollars. These penalties would apply to my son's counselors, doctors, hospital or anyone else with access or knowledge of his condition.

Amend a Broken Mind

Now I understood why the counselors, doctors and employees of hospitals got very cagy when I called and looked for information regarding my son and his situation. His present location in county jail, however, was different and unexpectedly, people talked to me about Sean's current behavior. They had no access to his medical information. But that turned out to be unnecessary. I found out that he was in the process of being evaluated by prison psychiatrists. I also found out that he was refusing to eat.

Sean's refusal to eat continued for 30 days at the jail. The mental health department called me and asked if this was Sean's usual behavior. I told them about his odd eating habits. Consequently, he was sent to Bridgewater State Hospital for further evaluation. The doctors at Bridgewater were able to get Sean to eat.

I did not visit with him in Middleton Jail or Bridgewater State hospital. However, I was in contact with his case workers. They were clearly anxious about growing signs that Sean's organs were beginning to shut down from lack of nutrition. They told me there was some success at Bridgewater getting Sean to eat when he was told a court order would be obtained that would allow them to restrain him and force feed him.

Historically, Bridgewater State Hospital did not have a good reputation. Before this writing, my only connection with Bridgewater was in the story Dick McCallum shared with me about his drinking years and his incarceration. He lived in the

13 – HOMELESS

"hole" at Bridgewater because of his violent behavior. Wikipedia describes Bridgewater State hospital as:

> *Located in southeastern Massachusetts, (it) is a state facility housing the criminally insane and those whose sanity is being evaluated for the criminal justice system. It was established in 1855 as an almshouse. It was then used as a workhouse for inmates with short sentences who worked the surrounding farmland. It was later rebuilt in the 1880s and again in 1974. Bridgewater State Hospital currently houses 309 inmates all of whom are adult males.*

In 1967 the documentary "Titicut Follies" was released. Filmmaker Frederick Wiseman observed the hospital for twenty-nine days, depicting the harsh treatment the inmates received by the correctional officers and how doctors were not aware of the proper treatment the inmates needed.

This was apparent with one inmate featured in the documentary. He was classified as a paranoid schizophrenic. He came to Bridgewater for medical testing but ended up being a resident there. He received powerful medication that made his mental state worsen as time progressed. He went to a review board to explain that he did not need to be at Bridgewater because the treatment he was receiving was not proper for his wellbeing.

His complaints were disregarded, and the board suggested stronger doses of tranquilizers. His case was not rare at

Amend a Broken Mind

Bridgewater. Probably precipitated by the "Titicut Follies", a 1967 legislative committee investigated allegations of "cruel, inhuman, and barbarous treatment". There were witnesses who were able to describe problems with the water and sewage systems, insufficient medical, kitchen, and recreational facilities.

As a result, in 1972 John Boone, the Massachusetts Commissioner of Corrections, closed the segregation unit at Bridgewater State Hospital because it required maintenance. Bridgewater's facilities were not suitable for the standard means of health and living. There were 90-year-old cell blocks which did not have any toilets.

Albert DeSalvo, who confessed to be the Boston Strangler, was an inmate at Bridgewater in 1967. He briefly escaped and was transferred to the maximum-security prison at Walpole.

Many of the prisoners at Bridgewater State Hospital were not criminally insane people. This is evident with a 29-year-old man who painted a horse in 1938. He was sent to Bridgewater for two years because he painted a horse with stripes to make it look like a zebra. He was a poor vendor whose occupation was selling fresh fruit. In order to appeal to the people and increase his sales, he painted the horse. He died at the facility at an old age.

There was a time at the Bridgewater State Hospital when many of the inmates were there long after their sentence date. In 1968 over 250 cases were reviewed of forgotten men at

13 – HOMELESS

Bridgewater. There were inmates that were at Bridgewater for over twenty-five years. Some inmates were transferred to Bridgewater from other jails and prison facilities and kept at Bridgewater for much longer than their sentences warranted.

In September 2016, Governor Charlie Baker announced the hospital would be moving away from a historical prison model and toward a more clinical approach to the treatment of the mentally ill. According to the plan, every inmate would receive an individualized plan of treatment within ten days of admission to the facility. Inmates who are on psychiatric medications would be seen by a psychiatrist on a timely basis and the facility would move to electronic health records. [10]

Fortunately, or because of the changes the Governor instituted, our experience with Bridgewater State Hospital was a positive one. As the day of Sean's jail sentence termination approached, the State Mental Health workers and doctors began preparing for a competency hearing for Sean. Sharon and I lived with a nagging fear that at the end of the 90-day sentence handed down in Probate court he would be released from care. If that happened, I suspected that Sean would disappear as he had in the past.

We would have to start the same scenario that we had just gone through over again. Fortunately, when he began to regain his health and his 90-day sentence was over he was committed to six months at Tewksbury Mental Hospital. To our great

AMEND A BROKEN MIND

relief he was placed in the care of the Massachusetts Department of Mental Health.

Unfortunately for Sharon and me, HIPAA laws now applied, and we could get no information on exactly where he was or what his treatment plan was. We did know what Sean's diagnosis was because of the testimony of the doctor at a commitment hearing. The commitment hearing was required to send him to Tewksbury once his 90-day contempt of court for nonpayment of alimony sentence had been served.

We were told by compassionate individuals who sensed our worry that Sean was in the locked ward at Tewkesbury Hospital in Tewksbury, Massachusetts. Tewksbury Hospital was authorized by an act of the Massachusetts General Court in 1852 to be an Almshouse. In the 1880s the then governor of the Commonwealth, Benjamin Butler, made headlines when he accused Tewksbury management and staff of a variety of abuses ranging from the venal, "financial malfeasance, nepotism, patient abuse, and theft of inmate clothing and monies", to the macabre, including "trading in bodies of dead paupers and transporting them for a profit to medical schools" and "tanned human flesh converted to shoes or other objects [...] from Tewksbury paupers." An investigation found no evidence of any truth to the allegations. However, Tewksbury's most famous child resident Anne Sullivan (Hellen Keller's companion) wrote:

13 – HOMELESS

Very much of what I remember about Tewksbury is indecent, cruel, melancholy, gruesome in the light of grown-up experience; but nothing corresponding with my present understanding of these ideas entered my child mind. Everything interested me. I was not shocked, pained, grieved or troubled by what happened. Such things happened. People behaved like that—that was all that there was to it. It was all the life I knew. Things impressed themselves upon me because I had a receptive mind. Curiosity kept me alert and keen to know everything.

Notwithstanding the findings of the official investigation, Tewksbury suffered a gruesome reputation. Management was changed, and the focus of the facility was changed. Today, it is a 370 bed Joint Commission accredited hospital. The hospital provides comprehensive treatment, care, and comfort to adults with medical and mental illnesses. The campus also holds drug and alcohol treatment facilities and other nonprofit health and recovery services. [11]

Sean was committed to Tewksbury for six months of treatment (a kindly court officer left the commitment open on the counter for me to read). Sharon and I went to visit Sean once we found where in the huge campus Sean was being held. Our first visit was not encouraging. He talked about the drinking water being recovered from the toilets and insisted that the food was recycled waste and he refused to eat or drink anything. Furthermore, Sean asked us to promise that we would tell no one where he was. I asked him, "Sean, do you know why you are here?"

He got thoughtful and replied, "I assume it's because I told the judge that I would not work. Connie probably has something to do with it. Do you know she hit me in the face the last time I saw her?"

"Yes", I said, "I was there."

"This place is bad for me. I need to get out of here. If they would just let me go to the woods, I wouldn't need any of the medication they are giving me."

"What are they telling you is your diagnosis?"

He answered, "Schizophrenia."

Sharon asked, "Will you sign the papers that will allow us learn about your treatment. We just want to make sure you are getting the help that you need."

"I'm not ready to do that." He responded.

Then I started to ask him if he missed his children, but he interrupted saying, "This visit is over. I need to rest."

He got up and walked away. Sharon and I followed. The ride home was quiet until I said, "You know, every time I visit him, I come away feeling very sad. The sadness lasts for a few days when I start to recover. By the time the next visit rolls around I feel pretty good until the visit is over. Then the cycle of sadness

13 – HOMELESS

and recovery repeats. What happened to the Sean we used to know?"

Time went on with Sharon and I visiting Sean every Wednesday. We met in a private visiting room. With Sean's approval, Sharon read the Bible out loud. We saw no improvement in his appearance or in his ability to communicate. He refused to shower. His fingernails and toenails remained uncut and were approaching two inches long. He refused to sleep on a bed or sit in a chair. Although, he talked less about the water being contaminated, he continued to complain about the food. In response, we brought rice and beans for him to eat when we visited. We also brought his favorite raw cashews. When we were not there, he would only eat peanut butter on whole wheat bread. It was obvious that he was not showering. After a while, at Sean's request, we brought a brush and some NO MORE TANGLES to our visit.

Sharon read the Bible as he sat on the floor in front of me, I attacked the mess on Sean's head by tugging and twisting his hair. I finally admitted that the mats of hair were not yielding to my efforts. The next visit Sean finally allowed us to cut the mats out. We were then able to brush out the rest of his hair. His counselor and doctor still refused to talk to us because of HIPAA, so we just kept coming to visit each week and we continued to feel the sadness every time we left the hospital.

Six months went by. It was the summer of 2017 and Sharon and I received a notice of a pretrial hearing for Sean's six-month commitment anniversary. The hospital needed a judge's order to hold Sean any longer. The hospital was looking for a one-year commitment this time. I went to the hearing and told the judge that I would like to be appointed Sean's guardian. The hospital requested a professional guardian be appointed. After some discussion, a trial date was scheduled, and we continued with our weekly visits still not knowing what exactly was going on at the hospital with Sean.

When the day came, Sean was ushered into the court room and sat at a table in front of the judge with his state appointed lawyer. Sharon and I were there as were Sean's doctor, hospital lawyer, and Sean's case manager. The hospital's lawyer was not prepared and had neglected to send the required documentation to Sean's lawyer. Consequently, the judge refused to hold the trial. However, Sean's lawyer and the hospital lawyer got together outside the court room with Sean and the doctor. During that meeting, Sean agreed to a temporary appointment of me as his guardian. The judge approved my appointment and another six-months commitment. Suddenly, the doctor, Sean's lawyer, and the hospital lawyer were all anxious to talk to me and share what was going on with Sean and his treatment at Tewkesbury.

I started attending bi-monthly case management meetings with Sean and his treatment team. At the first meeting I could attend I showed his team a photograph of Sean seven years prior when he was in a period of good mental health. He was part of the wedding party at his sister's wedding. In the picture he was

13 – HOMELESS

standing next to his girlfriend. Sean's two children, his youngest sister and I were also in the picture. We were dressed, "to-the-nines" in beautiful dresses and tuxedos. Everyone was smiling.

After passing around this picture the team looked at me. I said, "This photo was taken seven years ago."

I could say no more. The emotion welled up in me and I wept. I believe I was successful in my desire to give the doctors and the counselors a reference that clearly demonstrated the extent of Sean's fall to become the person they knew and treated every day. I also wanted them to see that, although Sean's recent mental recovery was encouraging, he had a long way to go.

Once I recovered, they thanked me for sharing the photo and, after a brief discussion where they encouraged me by saying they knew he had a long way to go and they would not release him prematurely, we turned to performing the business of getting Sean the services that he was due under the law. I signed the paperwork giving Sean health insurance. I signed the paperwork required for Sean to apply for disability benefits. I began the process to correct Sean's child support payments. I met with the doctor and learned that Sean's blood work showed that his organs were not functioning properly because of his refusal to eat properly. We also discussed the medication treatment plan and I found out what drugs Sean had been given during his time at Tewkesbury Hospital.

Amend a Broken Mind

On one visit six-months since the last court appearance, Sean asked Sharon and me to bring a pair of nail clippers so that he could cut his fingernails and toenails. A week later, at the team meeting, Sean was given authorization to go outside onto the hospital grounds in Sharon and my company during our visit. We would be able to hold the visit outside while Sharon and I walked around the grounds with him. We visited the Hospital vegetable garden and sat in the grass while I brushed his hair and Sharon read from the Bible. Laying in the grass luxuriating in the sun Sean said, "This feels so good. I cannot even explain how wonderful this feels."

Sharon and I looked at each other. I could sense her pleasure. This was like a ray of hope penetrating through the years of darkness – the first major improvement since Sean was sent to the care of Massachusetts Department of Mental Health.

It is now the end of October. Sixty-seven years have passed from the beginning of this story. It is difficult to exaggerate the feeling of hope the recent events have given Sharon and me. Simultaneously, there is an underlying anxiety. The doctors and counselors at the hospital are beginning to work with Sean to transition him to a group home. He signed the documents for a voluntary six-month commitment. He is now allowed to leave his locked ward alone for two hours each day. On our weekly visits, Sharon and I take him for eight hours at a time to the beach and a restaurant. At the restaurant he sits in a chair at a table, orders from a menu, and holds a normal conversation. He still looks like hell. However, he has a trial next week to

13 – HOMELESS

evaluate the need for me to continue as his guardian so that his transition to a more independent living situation can be made as smooth as possible.

We have been in this mental health game with Sean for about twelve-years and we have seen our best laid plans and Sean's best intentions come to naught time and time again. Right when we think the tide of events has turned the other shoe drops and we are back to the beginning again or as Sharon says, "We have a new normal."

Sharon and I have come to accept three things about Sean's illness. The first is that this is what mental illness looks like. In our situation, it is unlikely to change much in the time we have left on this earth. For Sean there will be relapses and recoveries with a "new normal" continually raising its ugly head. The second is that there is a strong indication that marijuana in partnership with a natural affinity triggered Sean's psychosis. The third is that being molested by Joey when Sean was young played a big role in his fragile emotional state later in his life.

I have also come to recognize that the words of Alcoholic Anonymous' promises have come to pass for me. Particularly the lines, "We will not regret the past nor wish to shut the door on it… No matter how far down the scale we have gone, we will see how our experience can benefit others."

When asked, I share my testimony of how God has worked in my life. I still feel some of the shame and embarrassment as I

AMEND A BROKEN MIND

speak to others. Nonetheless, I have come to know a new freedom and a new happiness.

In retirement I have been able to use my membership in the Massachusetts Bar to help others, my whole attitude and outlook on life has changed, my fear of people and economic insecurity have left me, I find that I intuitively know how to handle situations which used to baffle me, and finally, I have come to realize that God has done for me what I could not do for myself.

Nonetheless, God continues to answer my prayers. Although, not as dramatically as when I first started asking Him to help me. Regardless, I am grateful for the gift of faith that Dick gave me all those years ago when he said, "Chad, did you get down on your knees and ask God for help?" Life for me has been easier with faith in God. Vicissitudes seem to be less painfully dealt with since I received the give of faith. I can only find rest in God because I am personally powerless to amend a broken mind – a broken world.

I recovered from the insecurity that grabbed me after my boating accident. Yet, I have not put my boat in the water for five years. The drama and expense of Sean's illness has left me emotionally and physically exhausted. Maybe I'll get the Marian Gray in the water this weekend. Or maybe I'll just go to Plumb Island and walk on the beach with Sharon. I'll feel the wind on my cheeks, hear the waves crashing on the shore and delight in the sound of herring gull overhead. I will enjoy the

13 – HOMELESS

smell of the ocean while I wait patiently for further understanding and for the other shoe to drop.

Amend a Broken Mind

Bibliography

1. Alcoholics Anonymous (The Big Book): Page 35
2. Home School Legal Defense Association -- www.HSLDA.com: Page 48
3. https://vocal.media/beat/the-history-of-raves Blake O' Conner: Page 64
4. http://www.citypages.com/music/top-10-rules-of-the-rave-a-guide-to-underground-dance-party-etiquette-6648523 : Page 64
5. www.NAMI.org (National Alliance on Mental Illness): Page 75
6. https://www.heysigmund.com/marijuana-and-the-teenage-brain/
7. Hey Sigmund "Marijuana and the Teenage Brain" by Karen Young: Page 76
8. https://www.goodhousekeeping.com/life/a36953/ann-becker-son-ed-thomas-shooting/ by Ann Hinga Klein, March 28, 2016: Page 76
9. https://www.drugabuse.gov/publications/research-reports/marijuana/there-link-between-marijuana-use-psychiatric-disorders
10. NIH National Institute on Drug Abuse "Marijuana – Research Report Series": Page 76
11. https://www.City-Journal.com
12. "The Marijuana Delusion", article by Steven Malanga, Spring 2019: Page 77
13. http://www.Rainn.org

14. Article – "Sexual Assault on Men and Boys": Page 78
15. https://en.wikipedia.org/wiki/Bridgewater_State_Hospital
16. Wikipedia article Bridgewater State Hospital: Page 122
17. https://en.wikipedia.org/wiki/Tewksbury_Hospital
18. Wikipedia article Tewksbury Hospital: Page 124

www.ingramcontent.com/pod-product-compliance
Lightning Source LLC
Chambersburg PA
CBHW022103090426
42743CB00008B/700